The Children's Champion

George Müller

The Children's Champion

The Children's Champion: George Müller
© 2000 Irene Howat

Published by Christian Focus Publications Ltd,
Geanies House, Fearn, Tain, Ross-shire
IV20 1TW, Scotland, Great Britain

WEB PAGE:
www.christianfocus.com

Cover artwork is an accurate representation
of George Muller and of the children's home
Ashley Down, by Neil Reed.

Cover design by Owen Daily

Printed and bound in Great Britain
by Cox and Wyman, Cardiff Road, Reading

Introduction

George Müller lived a long life and this is a short book. His story doesn't leave time to be boring. An accomplished thief while still a small child, Müller's life changed completely when he was in his teens. His father didn't trust him with a penny, but God trusted him with over a million pounds, much of which was spent on feeding, clothing and providing a home for over ten thousand orphans.

Müller kept a journal, and this book is based on what he wrote in it. The situations described are true, but I created the conversations surrounding them. Quotations from his journal have been slightly adapted.

A very brief lesson in pre-decimal money is needed for the story to make sense. One pound was made up of two hundred and forty pennies, or twelve shillings. There were four crowns in a pound. And one pound equalled a sovereign. A guinea was worth one pound and one shilling. Based on the difference between a headmaster's salary in 1885 and 1999, one million pounds then would be worth approximately three hundred and eleven million pounds today.

I would like to thank my friend, Elsie Miller, for her helpful comments on the manuscript.

Irene Howat

Dedication
For Isabel, Ruth and Alison

Contents

It was 18th December 1821. George Müller was sixteen years old. And in those sixteen years he had learned to lie, steal, drink, gamble and lead an immoral life. His future looked bleak.

Apprentice thief

George picked up a sheet of paper and pushed his notebook to the side. Scribbling down a list of figures, he added it up, scored it out and shook his head. After thinking for a minute he grinned and wrote down several more figures. This time when he worked out their total he laughed aloud then copied them into his notebook. The boy was only just in time. Herr Müller opened the door and came in.

'Well,' his father asked, sitting opposite his son, 'have you got your pocket money sums done?'

'Yes Dad,' he said, handing the book over.

'That's good,' Herr Müller said, 'very good.'

George turned to the window to hide his grin from his father. Then, taking a deep breath, he turned round.

'Dad,' he began, 'why do you make me write down everything I spend my pocket money on? Fritz and Fredrick just laugh at me. It's not fair!'

Herr Müller smiled.

'Come, George,' he answered, 'sit down and I'll explain why.'

The boy's heart sank.

'Yuck!' he moaned inside himself. 'I want to go out to play and dad's going to talk for ages about money.'

'As you know,' his father began, 'in the course of my work I discuss money with many people. Some of them know exactly where every penny is, how much is invested, the exact figure they have in the bank, how much has been spent, and on what. These are the people I admire …'

'Fritz and Fredrick will go away if I don't get out soon,' George thought angrily.

'… and respect,' went on his father. 'And there are others whose accounts are a shambles. They know when I am coming to collect their taxes, and before I arrive they dash together some figures thinking I won't notice what they've done. But I can see through them every time.'

George had to feign a fit of coughing to cover up for the laughter that threatened to erupt.

'That is why,' his father continued, 'I have always given you and your brother more money than boys your age might expect. It is a good discipline to have money, to learn how to use it, and to keep accurate accounts. This little duty which I insist…'

Fixing his eyes on his father's face, George let his mind wander. He too was interested in money.

'I wish I'd lots and lots of money like the people Dad's talking about,' he thought. 'I'd buy a clockwork train set and a battalion of tin soldiers and lots of sweets and …'

'... so, George, the keeping of accounts is a necessity in every walk of life...'

'If Dad's so clever,' the boy wondered, 'why didn't he know I'd made up my pocket money sums?'

'... even Lutheran priests need to keep accounts, and as that is what your mother and I hope you will...'

'If I took some of Dad's tax money I could buy sweets and share them with Fritz and Fredrick. They wouldn't laugh at me then.'

George smiled at the thought.

'You find this amusing?' his father asked.

The boy jumped.

'No Dad.'

Rising to his feet, Herr Müller patted his son on the back, 'You'll continue with your pocket money sums then?'

The nine year old nodded dutifully.

Over and over again George slipped coins from his father's tax money into his pocket.

'Sit down, George,' Herr Müller demanded one day.

The boy sat, turned on an expression of absolute innocence, and waited.

'Did you, or did you not, remove money from my desk?'

George, whose deceit had made him a splendid actor, looked shocked at the thought.

Staring Herr Müller straight in the eye, he answered, 'No Dad, I didn't.'

'Come here.'

George walked across the room, ignoring the discomfort in his foot.

Maintaining his hurt expression he submitted to his father's search. Finding nothing in his pockets, or any other part of his clothing, Herr Müller sat back in his chair.

'Take off your shoes,' he ordered.

George bent forward and took off one shoe. His father felt his sock and found nothing.

'Easy now,' the boy said to himself, as he undid the lace in his other shoe and slipped his foot out. This sock was searched and nothing found. Very gently he pushed his toes back into the shoe.

'What was that?' Herr Müller bellowed, hearing the chink of coins.

George nearly fell over as his father snatched his shoe. And he could do nothing at all to prevent being found out.

Herr Müller looked at the coins as they tipped on to the floor.

'I suppose,' he said angrily, 'you did not notice these. And I suppose that you think I have not missed money in the past. From which I further suppose that you concluded your father was a fool. Instead of which, young man, you are the fool, taking the money I'd laid as a trap. And for your foolishness and dishonesty you are now going to be severely punished.'

After he had paid the painful price of his thefts George left the room. As he did so, father and son had very different thoughts. Herr Müller congratulated himself on teaching his son a lesson he would remember.

'I'll not get caught again,' the boy decided. 'I'll show him that I'm cleverer than he is!'

♦ ♦ ♦

One year later, in 1815, George and his brother were sent to Halberstadt, to the Cathedral Classical School there. This was the first step, as far as Herr Müller was concerned, in George's training for the ministry of the Lutheran church. But, while the boy studied enough to satisfy his teachers, there was nothing further from his mind than living the kind of life that would be expected of a trainee minister.

♦ ♦ ♦

'Oh my head,' George groaned as he wakened one Sunday morning.

'You're not the only one with a headache,' Hermann, his room-mate, growled. 'It took me hours to get back to sleep after you crashed in at 2 o'clock.'

'If you'd come with us you wouldn't be complaining. What a night we had,' remembered George from somewhere in the fuzziness of his brain. 'We played cards until our wrists were tired holding them then we gave our arms some exercise with beer tankards. And the jokes we told! There were some good looking girls around too. There was one with long blonde ...'

'Shut up, Müller, you're a disgrace! Anyone

would think you were twenty four instead of fourteen.'

George jumped to his feet. 'It's Sunday! I've got religious instruction!'

He looked in the mirror.

'I look like death warmed up,' he moaned, splashing cold water on his face and running his fingers through his hair.

Hermann glared at him. 'You've got a nerve, going to a confirmation class when you're hardly sober enough to have a religious thought in your head.'

George winked. 'The priest won't notice. His mind will be on his lunch.'

'Don't judge everyone by your own standards,' the other boy retorted.

'Phew, I'm glad that's over.' George slumped on his bed when he came back from his class. 'I've had enough religion to do me for a month!'

Hermann said nothing but nodded in the direction of the window.

George turned round.

'Father! What are you doing here?'

Herr Müller looked at his son. 'I've come to take you and your brother home.'

'Home? Why? What's wrong?'

George's father struggled to find words. 'It's your mother. She died last night. I'm taking you home to her funeral.'

The boy sat down in a daze.

'When did she die?' he asked.

'Last night.'

Suddenly George's night out flashed before his eyes. Had his mother died when he was drinking, or gambling, or was it when he had his arm round the blonde girl? He felt sick.

'Pack your things,' Herr Müller said. 'We'll have to hurry.'

Far from being brought to his senses by his loss, George Müller's behaviour grew worse. Just a few days before his confirmation he was guilty of immorality. And, two days later, when he had to confess his sins to a priest, he only gave him a twelfth of the money his father had sent for the priest's fee. On the Sunday after Easter 1820 George was confirmed, making a profession of faith in God, and taking the Lord's Supper. A little of the seriousness of the occasion affected him, enough to make him stay at home for the afternoon and consider his lifestyle.

Six weeks later George went on holiday to his father's sister's home in Brunswick. While he was there he met a young girl to whom he became very attached. Returning to his studies he found himself easily distracted. Playing the guitar or piano, reading novels and drinking in taverns all seemed much more enjoyable. 'I really must make the effort,' he told himself often, usually when he had run out of money and could not afford to go out anyway. But his resolutions came to nothing at all. So unwisely did he spend his money that he was once so hungry he stole food from a prisoner who was under house arrest in his lodgings.

'Father,' said George, when he was 16 years old, 'when you go to your new post at Schoenebeck, may I leave the Cathedral School and oversee the alterations on the house at Heimersleben?'

Herr Müller agreed to his son being there for a few months.

'Now I'll be able to live a better life,' the teenager thought. 'It was just the company I kept that led me astray.'

At first the work kept George busy, but after a short time he found he had not enough to do and he slipped into his old habits again. Then, having time on his hands, he became involved in the less savoury things that went on round about him. When his time at Heimersleben was nearly over he approached his father again.

'May I remain until Easter?' he asked. 'Dr Nagal would teach me Latin and I could take some pupils of my own.'

Knowing Dr Nagal, a local clergyman, to be a wise and learned man as well as a good friend, Herr Müller agreed.

'You will also act on my behalf,' he told his son, 'collecting the taxes in this area, giving receipts and keeping accurate accounts which you will send to me along with the money.'

George agreed, and it was his downfall. Accomplished thief that he was, the temptation to line his own pockets with his father's money was too much for him. He did collect the money. And he was careful always to give receipts. But much of it never reached his father. When asked why this one and that one had not paid, George would reply, with his usual innocence, that he didn't know why, all he knew was that they had not paid.

♦ ♦ ♦

George decided to have a November holiday. 'After all,' he reasoned, 'Father will never know. He's safely out of the way in Schoenebeck.'

He took as much money as he could lay hands on, told his tutor and pupils a pack of lies and headed for Brunswick, and the girl he had fallen in love with. Wishing to impress her he stayed in an expensive hotel, spent money like water, and wasted the days away. Just one week later he was penniless.

'I know what I'll do,' he decided, being unwilling to leave his girlfriend, 'I'll invite myself to stay at my uncle's home.'

But within a week his uncle had had enough. 'I do not wish you to remain here any longer,' he told his nephew.

Having packed his things, the teenager moved on. Incapable of learning a lesson, George moved into yet another expensive hotel where he spoiled himself for a further week.

'I should be grateful if you would settle your account,' said the hotel-keeper one day.

He was becoming a little suspicious. George made an excuse.

'Then perhaps,' the man went on, 'you could

give me your passport as a guarantee.'

'Passport,' thought George, 'not only have I no money, I haven't a passport either.'

'Yes, yes, of course,' he blurted out. 'I'll make arrangements to settle with you.'

But, as he could think of no way of paying his debt, George had to leave his best clothes as security and move out.

'Where do I go from here?' he wondered, walking out of Brunswick. 'How far will I need to walk before news of my debts will be left behind?'

For six miles he trudged along the road, stopping eventually at the inn in Wolfenbüttel. As the walk had made him hungry and thirsty he ate well and drank heartily, totally disregarding his empty pockets.

'I'd better make a run for it now before anyone becomes suspicious,' he decided two days later. He leaned out of his room window and considered his options.

'It's too high to jump down from here,' he decided, 'certainly in the dark, and I'd be seen if I tried during the day. I'm just going to have to bluff my way out of it.'

The following morning, in broad daylight, he walked casually across the inn's yard and out the other side.

'I'm nearly there,' he said to himself, 'take it gently.'

Glancing behind him and seeing nobody there, he broke into a run.

'Herr Müller,' a voice called. 'Herr Müller, come back!'

'I've had it if I go back, but they'll catch me if I go on, maybe even with the dog.' George thought quickly. 'There's nothing else for it, I'm done for.'

The innkeeper came out to meet him.

'Going off without settling your account, were you?'

George considered his answer. Would he try to bluff his way out, or did he for once have to confess that was exactly what he had intended doing. Deciding to trust the innkeeper's good nature he explained that he had no money on him. But the innkeeper was not good-natured. He had George arrested and escorted to the police between two soldiers. After three hours of questioning he was put in prison.

'How did I get myself into this mess?' he asked himself, as his cell door clanged shut behind him.

It was 18th December 1821. George Müller was sixteen years old. And in those sixteen years he had learned to lie, steal, drink, gamble and lead an immoral life. His future looked bleak.

———————

'Well, hello! You going my way?' a young man's voice called to George from behind him. 'Depends which way you're going.' George replied, not looking round. 'From bad to worse,' came the answer, as the owner of the voice drew alongside. George laughed. 'That's good! That's the direction I'm going in too.'

———————

From bad to worse

'I can't eat that!' George growled, looking with disgust at the meat, bread and vegetables the prison guard held out to him.

'You've no cause for complaint,' the guard grunted. 'The others only have bread and veg. It's there if you want it, and there will be nothing else till morning.'

George looked down at the plate then up at the guard.

'You'd best eat it,' the man said not unkindly, as he drew the door shut behind him.

George heard the key turn on the other side, and with the sound of its being removed from the door his heart sank. His stomach rumbled with hunger but the smell of the cheap meat put him off even tasting it. He picked up the bread which had been soaking in the water the meat was cooked in. The lump of bread was soggy. Holding it up George looked at it, and as he did the weight of the sodden bread broke it in two. Half of it fell on the floor at his feet. Putting the bit that was left back on the plate he screwed the sodden lump into the floor.

'That's all it's fit for,' he said aloud, kicking the plate into the corner of the cell.

'You can have it,' he said to any mice who happened to be there. 'It's only fit for the likes of you.'

Never had George spent a longer night. In his half sleep he heard the snores and groans of the other prisoners.

'I wonder what they are in here for?' he asked himself. 'I don't suppose they only tried to get off without paying their bills.'

George smiled.

'I nearly did it though. Another two minutes and I would have been away.'

His mind wandered.

'Now, if I were to find myself in the same situation again, what would I do? I suppose I could give some excuse for going away for an hour or two. They'd be less likely to think I was running away if I spoke to them first. Uncle might come in useful. They would know his name, and I could say I was going to visit him.'

George thought about that.

'No,' he decided, 'that wouldn't work. When I didn't come back they would go to Uncle, he would tell Father, and I would pay for that dearly. How else could I get off with it?'

His scheming was interrupted by a scream.

'I didn't do it,' a tortured voice protested. 'I didn't kill Gretel. It was an accident. I didn't mean to do it.'

George shivered.

'A murderer! There's a murderer in here!'

He shook with both cold and fear as he turned over and willed himself to fall asleep.

'You look as if you have had a bad night,' the guard observed, 'and a hungry one,' he added, looking at the plate in the corner.

'I heard screams,' George said. 'Is there a man in here who's a murderer?'

'That's what he's accused of, yes,' the guard answered. 'His daughter got the worst of his drunken rage and did not survive the experience.'

'And the others...?'

'The usual crowd: thieves, rapists, murderers, the lot. Just what you'd expect in a prison.'

The guard picked up the plate.

'You'll be ready to eat whatever you're given today, young man. More's the fool you were to leave this. Men have killed for less.'

With that the door swung shut. Having spent the longest night of his life, George discovered it was to be followed by the longest day.

'I'll go mad if I've to stay here much longer,' he thought. 'What am I to do with myself? The window's hardly big enough to let light in, there's no way I could get out of it even if it didn't have iron rails across it. And the door? Never was a door as firmly shut as this one is,' he decided, remembering the sound of the key rasping in the lock. 'And I can't even try to bribe the guard because I don't have a single penny to my name. But I've got to do something to stop me going out of my mind.'

Pulling himself to his feet he walked briskly round his cell, first clockwise then in the other direction.

'I feel sick,' he moaned aloud, after walking for what seemed ages, 'going round in circles on an empty stomach doesn't work.'

'You'll eat this then,' said the guard, who had heard him as he approached the door.

Holding out his hand for what he expected would be meat, vegetables and potatoes, George found he was given only bread and water.

'I need something to do,' he pleaded with the guard. 'Can you give me something to do, or a book to read, any book?'

'You've got it wrong, young man,' came the reply, 'this is a prison not a workshop or library. You think you're smart,' he went on, 'but you've a lot to learn. You'll learn it quickly, shut up in here,'

Left alone, George looked at his bread.

'At least it's not soaked in brine this time,' he said, breaking off a bit and eating it. He spat it out.

'Never, ever have I tasted bread like that! It's sour ... foul ... only fit for pigs!'

Having downed the whole tankard of water to get rid of the taste, he suddenly realised his mistake. The comfort of his upbringing had not prepared him for a small prison cell which had to act as bedroom, living-room and toilet. Everything in him rebelled at the squalor of it.

'If I can't get out,' he decided, 'I've got to

have something to do. I can't spend my days looking at a locked door, a barred window and a foul pail in the corner.'

'May I have a Bible?' he asked the guard when he came with the vegetables which made up his dinner.

'A Bible? Religious, are you?' the guard laughed . 'I didn't think you were from all I've heard about you.'

'Please get me a Bible,' George pleaded, thinking that, if nothing else, a Bible would be long enough to keep him reading for however long he was in prison.

'Needing food for your soul as well as your body,' the officer sneered, noticing the leftover lunch time bread. 'You'll soon be so hungry that you'll eat whatever you're given.'

Mustering up all his best manners, George swallowed hard and spoke again.

'Thank you for the meal. Please could you see if you could get me a Bible? I would be most grateful.'

'A gentleman are we? Well, is life not full of little surprises. A Bible? I'll see what I can do.'

The smell of the vegetables mixed with the smell of urine made the boy feel sick. He tried to eat but the food in his mouth seemed to go round and round, not wanting to be swallowed at all. With a great deal of effort he managed to take a little.

'This is hell,' he moaned, lying down on his mat. 'Hell can't be any worse than this.'

'Who's that!' George shouted when his cell door scraped open in the middle of the night. He could see nothing, but in his mind's eye he could see the murderer.

A face appeared above a low lit lamp. George gasped. The light hit the face on the chin, shining through the edges of a beard, highlighting the underside of a man's jowls, rendering him in a grotesque mix of light and shade.

'Shut up, or you'll have the whole jail awake!' commanded a voice in the darkness.

'Running scared are you?' sneered someone else from beside the cell door which clanged shut.

'What... what do you want? Who are you?' George's voice quavered over the words. His mouth was dry with fear, and he shook.

'Routine check, sir,' the first man mocked. He held the lamp up to the window, so giving George a view of his companions. All three were prison guards. By the light of the lamp they checked the window bars.

'Wouldn't want you to run off now, would we?' the lamp carrier grinned menacingly at the boy.

'Well he won't do that,' one of the other two said, 'at least not through these window bars.'

'Sleep well!' laughed the last guard to go out the doorway. 'Sweet dreams.'

'It puts them in their place, giving them the fright of their life,' he heard one say to the others as the door closed. George slumped against the wall, shaking with rage and fear.

'Did you get me a Bible?' George asked next morning, taking a bite of bread before the guard had time to reply.

'So you've discovered hunger at last,' the man laughed. 'No I don't have a Bible for you. You'll have to make do with food for your body. I've got none for your soul if you have one.'

'Please,' the boy pleaded, 'please will you try to get one for me?'

Laughing, the guard drew the door shut behind him and locked it on the outside.

'He said that a murderer was in prison, but he didn't say he was in the next cell. I wonder who is.' George knocked on the thick wooden wall that divided him from his neighbour.

'Hello!' he shouted, knocking again, 'Is there anybody there?'

'Yes,' a voice, dulled by the wood, replied. 'Who are you?'

'Müller,' George answered. 'And you?'

They shouted to each other, the company of his unseen friend keeping George from despair.

'Can the prisoner next door come in with me?' he asked the guard a day or two later. 'It will give you an empty cell.'

'And he would be better company than the Bible I didn't get,' George thought to himself, 'and a lot more fun.'

◆ ◆ ◆

'Come in, and welcome!' George greeted his fellow prisoner.

'Sorry the accommodation is third class,' he grinned. 'It's the best I've got at the moment.'

The man told George about other prisons he had been in, by way of comparing them to this one.

'And you,' he asked, 'where have you done time?'

Wanting to be one up on his new companion, George spun a lengthy yarn.

'Prison? I've never been inside before. Always been too clever you see. Want to hear how I've done it?'

Lie followed lie, and his stories became more outrageous as time went on.

'Oh be quiet, would you!' sniped his fellow prisoner.

That's gratitude for you,' complained George. 'I invite you into my cell, entertain you with my stories, give you the benefit of all my experiences and tell you the tricks of my trade. And you tell me to be quiet.... you've a cheek, you have.'

'I said, be quiet,' his companion's voice was menacing. 'Be quiet before I quieten you with my fist.'

The silence that fell was thick, and it hung in the cell for days.

♦ ♦ ♦

On 12 January 1822, the prison door opened and the guard signalled to George to come out. Turning to his companion to say a final word, George was met only by the back of his head.

'Where am I going?' the boy asked.

'Home to a beating, I hope, you deserve no less.'

'I'm going home!' George laughed aloud, 'Home! Home!'

'If your father has an ounce more sense than you, you'll be black and blue when he sees you.'

'And let this be a lesson to you, young man,' the Governor said. 'You're a disgrace to your father and to the memory of your poor mother.'

'But I don't understand,' George said.

'Nor do you deserve to, but I'll tell you all the same,' the Governor continued. 'After your trial the Commissioner wrote to your uncle informing him of your crime and of your circumstances. Your uncle, wise man, wanted nothing to do with you and said you were your father's responsibility not his. When he heard about you, your father, a generous man of whom you are not worthy, sent enough to pay your debt at the inn, your maintenance here and your travelling expenses home.'

George grinned.

'And I'd be a happier man if I were to see tears of gratitude on your face rather than that stupid grin. Now, get home to your father, and keep out of trouble.'

George swaggered out of the prison gate. The Governor, watching from his window, shook his head.

Walking along the road, George took deep breaths of freedom. Never had the air felt so clear. The smell of urine, which had disgusted him for nearly a month, faded into a memory as his clothes were freshened in the breeze.

'He's welcome to my cell,' George said to himself, thinking of his prison companion.

'After my kindness to him! And if he thinks I'll deliver his message to his wretched sister before I head for home, he has another thing coming!'

George strode on, his muscles relaxing as he went.

'Well, hello! You going my way?' a young man's voice said from behind him.

'Depends which way you're going.' George replied, not looking round.

'From bad to worse,' came the answer, as the owner of the voice drew alongside.

George laughed. 'That's good! And that's the direction I'm going in too.'

Each had found a companion suited to his taste. And they set out together along the road. Time passed quickly as they walked, and George was sorry to say goodbye when his fellow traveller left him at a crossroads several miles later.

George Müller

———————

'Are any of you willing,'
the speaker concluded,
'to answer God's call to
work among the Jews?'
'I'll go,' said Müller. 'If
God will use me, I'll go.'

———————

New beginnings

'It's good to be home,' George said to himself when he arrived back at Heimersleben. 'And Father's not here - so a drink to celebrate.'

Two days later he could neither celebrate nor sit, so severely beaten had he been by his father.

'You are coming back to Schoenebeck with me.'

'But...'

'There are no buts. You've shown what you can do with your life when you're left to your own devices. Now, sit down and listen!'

Herr Müller's son sat.

'You will study under a tutor, and at the same time take pupils and earn your keep. What subjects are you fit to teach?'

George thought before answering, 'Latin, French, arithmetic and German grammar.'

'That should bring in enough,' Herr Müller said. 'We'll review the situation at Easter time.'

♦ ♦ ♦

'Well,' George thought to himself three months later, 'Father has nothing to complain about. I've never worked so hard in my life.'

'Father,' he said one day in April, 'you said we would review my situation at Easter.'

Herr Müller nodded. 'What do you have to say for yourself?'

That took George by surprise: he had expected his father to do the talking.

'Eh? My tutor's pleased with my studies. And the pupils' parents are pleased with theirs.'

Herr Müller smiled. 'You've improved a lot, I'll grant you that. I think you are now ready to go to Halle to sit your examinations.'

'Halle!' George gulped. 'I'd do better if you allowed me to keep at my studies and tutoring until Michaelmas.'

Father looked at his son. 'A month or two more at home can only do him good,' he thought. 'Till Michaelmas,' he agreed. 'Then to Halle.'

'Thank you, Father,' George said. He left the room. Closing the door behind him, he rubbed his hands gleefully and punched into the air.

♦ ♦ ♦

'I wish you well,' Herr Müller said, patting George on the back as he left to sit his exams. 'And I hope I will soon be the proud father of a senior pupil at Halle, and before long the parent of a university student there!'

The young man set off.

'He's learned his lesson at last,' his father thought.

'Fooled again!' George grinned, changing direction and taking the road to Nordhausen. 'No way am I gong to Halle. I know too many of the university students. They'd make a fool of my still being at school. Now .... how am I going to pull this off?'

That gave him plenty to think about as he travelled. He was still thinking about it on the return journey.

'Father,' he said, 'I passed!'

'Well done,' Herr Müller said warmly. 'Well done.'

'There's a lot to do before I leave,' the boy tried to escape before he was asked awkward questions.

But awkward questions there were, and George lied his way out of each one.

◆ ◆ ◆

'Are you ready, my boy?' Herr Müller asked, the day before George was due to go.

'I've just some last minute things to do.'

'I'll leave you to it then,' he turned to leave.

'Dad?'

'Yes, my boy?'

'It's about Halle. It's really not the place for me.'

Herr Müller sat down heavily. 'What do you mean?'

'After a great deal of consideration regarding Halle,' George tried to sound adult, 'I came to the conclusion that I should be examined at

Nordhausen and finish my schooling there.'

Herr Müller's eyes narrowed and his mouth twitched dangerously.

George made the most of his father's momentary confusion.

'And that was confirmed to me when I sat my examination there. Nordhausen is just the kind of place that will inspire me to study.'

Finding his voice, Herr Müller put it to good use, telling his son in no uncertain terms what he thought of his deceit. A long and heated argument followed but George remained unmovable.

When he left for Nordhausen it was with his father's words ringing in his ears. 'You had better do well. For your next move is to Halle.'

♦ ♦ ♦

'Who's the perfect student?' George asked himself as he considered his first term's good results. 'Haven't I done well? Two and a half years at Nordhausen and not a soul knows the real George Müller. Why? Because I'm the best liar in Prussia![1] A first class, prize-winning liar! Even I don't always know when I'm telling a lie, I'm so convincing!'

'Now to apply my superior mind to the little matter of my considerable debts ... I've got it! What a good idea. Well done me!'

'Look at this, fellows,' George held out his hand, showing some money to his friends. 'See what my Father sent.'

[1] Prussia. Now Northern Germany.

'That's the scene set.' He smirked when they left. 'Now a little patience.'

♦ ♦ ♦

'..and the money my father sent has been taken...' George concluded breathlessly.

The director looked hard at him. 'Start at the beginning and tell me exactly what happened.'

George did. 'I received money from my father and I put it in my trunk and locked it. When I came back I found the lock broken ... and the money...,' he swallowed hard and mopped his brow, '... is gone.'

Müller paused as if to collect himself. 'My friends will tell you it's true.'

George's friends, not realising that he was making fools of them, clubbed their money together and gave him the amount he claimed he had lost. The director, who until then had given his student the benefit of many doubts, never felt as kindly towards him again.

♦ ♦ ♦

'That was decent of the boys to make up the money you lost,' someone said to young Müller a few days later. George felt uncomfortable.

'Especially as they've left themselves short,' his companion went on.

Fingering the ill-gotten money in his pocket, the boy muttered his agreement, turned and left.

'How could I do that?' he asked himself as he slouched down the street. 'They're my mates.'

'Müller!' some voices called from across the road. 'We're going for a walk. Coming with us?'

It was the friends he had swindled.

'No thanks!" he shouted back. 'I've things to do.'

'See you later!' they chorused.

'I can't face them,' George thought miserably. 'What a mess I'm in. Some minister I'll make. What good could I be to a congregation? I can't even sort myself out.'

♦ ♦ ♦

It was with a sense of relief that soon afterwards he left his school days behind and went, with good intentions, to the University of Halle. But his good intentions melted in the summer sun. Müller lived as wild a life as his money allowed. But there was a difference George no longer enjoyed it.

♦ ♦ ♦

'Beta!' Müller called across the crowded pub.

Beta looked round at the sound of his name. 'Müller! What a surprise!' he said, squeezing on to the bench beside his former class-mate. 'It's good to see you.'

George laughed. 'And you.'

That night the two young men lay in their beds thinking opposite thoughts.

'That's a stroke of luck,' Müller comforted himself. 'Beta's a good guy. He's just the man to help me keep on the straight and narrow.'

'I should learn a thing or two about enjoying

myself now,' smiled Beta to himself. 'No more religious stuff for me. From now on it's beer, women and whatever else takes my fancy. And what better teacher than Müller.'

And they both fell asleep happy.

♦ ♦ ♦

That summer Müller, Beta and some friends headed to Switzerland on holiday. George supplied the passports, obtained through letters they forged, and they sold their books to pay for the trip. He was also in charge of the cash, all the better to steal from. Gambling ate at their money, and drinking swallowed more of it. What was left was spent on pretty girls who had no more sense than to keep company with the young fools. Penniless, the students returned to Prussia and separated, each going home until the beginning of term. Having discovered the excesses that he had let himself in for, Beta found that he couldn't live with his conscience. Confessing to his father the truth about the Swiss holiday, he took his advice and discussed his problems with Dr Richter, a Christian friend of his father's. When he went back to university he took with him a letter from Dr Richter, introducing him to a man named Wagner.

♦ ♦ ♦

'What are you doing tonight?' Müller asked, as he and Beta walked along a street in Halle in November 1925.

'I usually visit Herr Wagner on a Saturday.'

'Wagner? Do I know him?'

Beta smiled at the thought. 'I don't think he's quite your type.'

Müller stopped and looked at his friend. 'Explain yourself,' he demanded.

Swallowing hard, Beta told the story of the last few weeks.

'... So I took the letter to Wagner. He treated me like a real friend! And it turned out that he has a meeting in his house every Saturday.'

'A meeting? What kind of meeting?'

'We read the Bible, sing and pray. And Herr Wagner reads a sermon.'

The two walked on in silence.

'That's what I need,' George thought to himself. 'That's what I've been looking for and never finding.'

'I'm going with you,' he said firmly.

His friend was apologetic. 'They're not your kind of people.'

'You'll come for me?' Müller begged.

Beta looked embarrassed and undecided. Turning to his friend he caught a look of urgency in his eyes.

'All right,' he agreed. 'If that's what you want.'

♦ ♦ ♦

'I'm sorry to come without an invitation,' George said on meeting Herr Wagner.

The man smiled, 'Come as often as you please; house and heart are open to you.'

Müller watched all that went on and listened to every word. After a hymn was sung, a man named Kayser, who was a missionary in Africa, knelt and prayed. George was amazed! Kayser prayed without reading from a book, using just his own words! And he was kneeling ... bowed down before God, like someone approaching a king. All this was new to George and made a profound impression on him. More was to follow. Kayser read first from the Bible, then from a written sermon, something that was against the law in Prussia unless the preacher was ordained by the church. And at the close of the meeting Herr Wagner prayed for those present.

'I couldn't pray as well,' George thought to himself, 'though I am much cleverer than him.'

When he had arrived at Herr Wagner's home, Müller had been apprehensive and unsure of himself, searching for something, but not quite sure what. But just a few hours later, as the house door closed behind them, he felt different, very different. He had found what he was looking for: forgiveness for the sins that had blackened his past, and a new and living relationship with a living Saviour. It was a happy young man who walked home that night.

◆ ◆ ◆

'I challenge you to a drinking match,' Müller's friend Gunter said when he met him the following afternoon.

'No thanks,' replied George.

His friend grinned. 'Got a better offer?'

'I certainly have. Want to hear about it?'

Gunter nodded. 'When I saw you and Beta heading off together last night I knew you were up to something. Have you found a new drinking den? Or was it a pretty girl?'

George swallowed hard. 'We went to a meeting together.'

His friend's eyebrows rose. 'And....?'

'And I discovered that Jesus is alive and that he loves me,' Müller said, his voice shaking with a mixture of excitement at his discovery and fear at what his friend would say.

'You must have been as drunk as a sailor on weekend leave!' Gunter laughed.

George looked his friend in the eye and said, 'I've never been more sober. And that's the way I'll stay.'

Grinning, from ear to ear Gunter slapped Müller on the back. 'We'll see about that,' he laughed, walking off in the direction of the pub. 'I'll leave you to your prayers.'

George watched him go. A little way down the road Gunter met up with a group of young men. Minutes later they dissolved in laughter.

'You'll be in the pub with us before the night's out,' one shouted to Müller.

'It'll pass,' another called. 'You'll get over it.'

'Say a prayer for us,' laughed a third.

Then Gunter's voice rose above the others. 'That's right!' he roared. 'Pray that I'll win at cards tonight.'

'God help me,' George said aloud. 'God help me not to sink to that depth again.'

And he never did.

♦ ♦ ♦

'Do you mind me coming here as often as I do?' Müller asked Herr Wagner some weeks later.

'Mind?' The man smiled graciously. 'Not at all.'

'I've such a lot to learn,' George explained. 'And you're so good at answering my questions.'

'Is there something worrying you?' his friend asked, looking at the young man's sad expression.

Taking a letter from his pocket, Müller handed it to Wagner. He read it slowly.

'Did you expect your father to be pleased you'd become a Christian?' the man asked.

'I suppose I did.'

'Then this must have come as a shock to you.'

George nodded. 'It's so bitter.'

Handing the letter back, Herr Wagner said, 'Your father chose how to reply, but you can choose how you react to his letter. It can depress you or inspire you to pray.'

Müller's eye's lit up, perhaps with tears, 'I know which I'll choose,' he said emphatically.

That night he stuck the letter under his pillow to remind him to pray, and to keep praying.

♦ ♦ ♦

'We need more missionaries,' the speaker at Herr Wagner's meeting was emphatic. 'Men and women to speak for the Lord Jesus.'

That was the night George knew that God was calling him to mission work.

'And there is an area of special need,' the speaker went on, 'to take the good news of Jesus to his own people, the Jews. They still walk in darkness unaware that the light of the Gospel is shining.'

The sadness of that situation hit George's heart.

'Are any of you willing,' the speaker concluded, 'to answer God's call to work among the Jews?'

'Sir, I'll go,' said Müller. 'If God will use me, I'll go.'

But first he had to get his father's permission.

♦ ♦ ♦

His visit home went well at first but the atmosphere changed when George explained his plans.

'Mission work!' Herr Müller bellowed. 'Do you know how much I've spent on your education to get you a good living in a church here in Prussia, so that I could spend my old age in comfort with you?'

It was with a heavy heart that George left. But the journey gave him time to think.

'If God has work for me to do,' he decided, 'he'll provide all I need. I wonder how he'll do it.'

He didn't have to wait long to find out.

♦ ♦ ♦

'I think I know just the person you're looking

for,' the Professor of Divinity told some visiting Americans. 'I'm sure he would give you German tuition.'

A meeting was arranged.

'We'll pay you well,' the Americans told Müller. 'If you'll teach us well.'

George smiled. 'I'll do my best.'

'When can we start?' asked one of the visitors.

'Tomorrow at eleven?' Müller suggested.

The Americans agreed. 'We'll have our pencils sharpened,' one commented with a grin.

That was the first in a series of remarkable happenings which culminated on 10th February 1829 when George left his father's home for England, to do six months' training for work with The London Society for promoting of Christianity among the Jews. Five weeks later, on 19th March, he landed in London. Although he knew enough Latin, Greek, French and German to be excused classes in them, his English was poor. He studied Hebrew in the seminary and practised English when he could.

♦ ♦ ♦

'Dear Friend,' George wrote to one of his Prussian friends, 'I have heard of a most remarkable man. He is a Mr Groves, a dentist from Exeter. Here, as at home, dentists earn a good living. Mr Groves has given up his dentistry, and the salary that went with it, to go with his wife and children to work as a missionary in Persia[2] - with no salary at all! It thrills me to think of it!' Something told Müller that he would not forget Anthony Norris Groves and what he had done.

Just a few weeks later George was in no fit state for writing anything at all. He was so ill he thought he might die. He prayed through every possibility.

'Lord, if you want me to get better, please let the medicine help. But if not, I pray you will soon take me home to heaven. Or if it is your will, Lord, to use a longer illness, do what seems best to you.'

Two weeks later he was fit to be out of his bed.

'I think you should go to the country to recover,' a friend suggested.

'It's the best thing you could do,' his doctor told him on his next visit.

It was to Teignmouth in Devon he went. A few days after his arrival he attended a local service and was impressed by the preaching of a Scotsman, Henry Craik.

The man with whom Mr Craik was staying came up to George and asked 'Will you come and spend some time with us?'

Accepting the invitation, George moved to Exmouth and spent ten days getting to know Henry and finding in him a real friend.

♦ ♦ ♦

On his return to London, Müller felt increasingly that although he wanted to tell Jews about the Lord, he didn't only want to tell Jews. He came to the conclusion that he should break his connection with the Society and, with good will on both sides, that is what happened. Two days before the year ended George went back to the home in Exmouth in which he had found such a welcome a few months before. As the new year and the new decade dawned, George Müller must have wondered what it held for him.

'Yesterday morning I drove with my father to Halbertstadt, where we said a tearful goodbye. ... I found myself again on the road to Brunswick, which I had travelled twice in the service of the devil, and now I was travelling in the name of Jesus. It was a strange feeling, passing the inn at Wolfenbüttel, where I'd run from the innkeeper right into the arms of the law!'

No pay, please

'It takes my breath away when I think how detailed God's plans are for our lives,' George told Henry Craik, in April 1830.

'I know what you mean,' his friend replied.

'Think of it,' George went on, 'I was born in Prussia and you in Scotland but God wanted us to be together. So what did he do? He took me out of an evil pit of my own making then allowed me to fail my medical so that I didn't have to do military service so allowing me to come to London as a trainee missionary. When I was there he made sure I heard about Anthony Groves. Then he brought me to Teignmouth where I met you.'

'It's just as remarkable from my point of view,' Henry agreed. 'After I was converted when I was a student at St Andrew's University, I prayed God would lead me to the job he wanted me to do. That turned out to be tutoring in the Groves' home in Exeter which brings us to our meeting when you came to church and I was preaching.'

George was silent for a minute. 'I believe,' he said, ' that God has a plan for our lives that involves us being together. Why else would he bring me from Prussia and you from Scotland to meet here?'

'First things first,' said Henry, looking at the time, 'we'll have to go. We can't have Mr George Müller late for his first service as pastor of Ebenezer Chapel, Teignmouth.'

◆ ◆ ◆

'What a year this has been,' George Müller said to the young woman at his side.

Although it was October, it was just warm enough to sit outside and watch the ducks.

She smiled. 'A happy one I hope.'

Looking at Mary, his wife of two weeks, George replied. 'None more so. Ten months ago I was a student for Jewish missions. In April God led me to be pastor here. And to crown it all,' he took her hand and kissed it, 'he gave me a lovely and godly wife. And,' he went on, 'from my long experience of married life, that is fifteen days and three and a half hours, I've come to the conclusion that marriage is one of his most precious gifts of all.'

Mary blushed. 'And I thought your interest in my family was because of my brother!'

'It was,' George admitted. 'When I first heard of Anthony Groves I was quite bowled over by his willingness to give us his income and serve the Lord without pay, believing that God would provide for all his needs, especially as he had a wife and family.'

'And God has never left them in need,' his wife said. 'Not once.'

Mary's hand was still in her husband's. He stroked it gently.

'I've been praying about our finances,' George said.

'Yes?'

'Ebenezer Chapel gives me £55 a year,' he went on. 'But I'm becoming convinced that we should not accept it. The more I think about it, the more I'm sure that Anthony is right. That we should not accept payment but rather look to the Lord to provide for us, just like them,' he added, pointed to some ducks that were pecking at the pond weed.

'I agree,' Mary said. 'And I don't agree without thinking about it. It has been on my mind and in my prayers ever since Anthony told me what he had decided to do.'

George bowed his head.

'Are you all right?' his wife asked.

He nodded. 'Yes,' he said, in a voice husky with emotion, 'I'm just overwhelmed at God's goodness in giving me such a wife as you are.'

George recorded what happened a few weeks later. 'Our money was reduced to about eight shillings. When I was praying with my wife in the morning the Lord brought this to my mind, and I was led to ask him for money. Four hours later we were with a sister at Bishopsteignton, and she said to me, "Do you need any money?" I said, "I told the brethren when I gave up my salary that I would for the future only tell the Lord about my needs." She replied, "But he has told me to give you some money." ... I turned the conversation to other subjects, but when I left she gave me two guineas.'

'Between Christmas and New Year, our money was reduced to a few shillings. I asked the Lord for more. A few hours later a brother from Axminster gave us a sovereign.' So ended 1830 and the Müllers' life of dependence on God began. But it was not always easy, as George discovered when 1831 was a few days old.

'On the evening of January 8th ... for about five minutes I was tempted to think it was no use trusting the Lord in this way.... When I returned to my room God had again supplied our needs. For a sister in the Lord from Exeter had come to Teignmouth and brought us £2 4s.'

Six months later he wrote in his journal, 'A shoulder of mutton and a loaf were sent to us anonymously. ... Whilst we have sometimes not had one single penny left; and we have been down to our last loaf of bread, we have never sat down to a meal without it being provided for us'

'Listen to this, Mary,' Müller said, unfolding a letter. 'It's from Henry Craik. He is visiting Bristol.' 'My dear Brother, I have now been here two weeks and have preached several times. There is so much to do here for the Lord. A harvest of souls is waiting to be gathered in. I pray God that he will send men to do that work. Would you join me in Bristol and see for yourself what there is to do?'

Pausing, George looked at his wife.

'If the Lord wants you to go, you must go,' she said. 'And he will provide the coach fare for the journey.'

'It will only be for a few days, then I will be home.'

Mary looked steadily at her husband as he folded the letter and put it back in his pocket. She knew that he felt their time in Teignmouth was coming to an end.

'I wonder ....' she said.

'When the time comes for us to leave here, my dear, our Lord will show us which coach to take.'

And he did. Within a month Müller and Craik were sure that Bristol was where they should be, and that they should be working together. Gideon Chapel was prepared to accept them under their rather unusual terms. The two pastors were not to be tied to that church but free to preach wherever they felt God led them. And they were to have no regular salaries, both relying on the Lord to give them everything they needed.

'We'll miss the people of Teignmouth,' Mary said, looking out of the coach window at the town in the distance.

Her father nodded, 'I'm sure you will. God has blessed your first home together.'

'And he'll bless our second one too,' George smiled reassuringly at his wife.

Taking her eyes off Teignmouth, Mary looked in the direction of Bristol.

'And I'm looking forward to seeing how he does it,' she said, and meant it.

It was 23rd May 1832. On the following day Henry Craik left his congregation in Shaldon. He was also on a coach bound for Bristol.

Soon after arriving in the city a member of Gideon Chapel paid the rent for Bethesda Chapel, so that they might have the use of it too. The first service was held there on 6th July. And on the 13th, George noted in his journal, 'Today we heard of the first cases of cholera in Bristol.'

The disease progressed.

'August 14th We set apart today for prayer concerning the cholera.'

'August 17th From six to eight o'clock this morning we had a prayer meeting about the cholera.'

'August 24th This morning a sister in the Lord who lived just fifty yards away was taken ill with cholera. She died this afternoon ... Great numbers die daily in this city ... Just now, ten in the evening, the funeral bell is ringing, and has been ringing for most of the evening. It rings almost all the day.'

'It's just about time,' Mary told her husband. 'The baby will come any day now.'

The funeral bell tolled outside. 'It's so sad,' George replied. 'When so many are dying we are waiting for our child to be born.'

'There are babies among the cholera victims,' Mary reminded him.

He nodded. 'I know that. But we're in the

Lord's hands.'

'And we're safe there,' she agreed. 'But sometimes I fear for our little one. These are terrible times to be born.'

George put his arm round her shoulder.

'Mary,' he said. 'Life and death are in God's hands. We'll have our child for as long as God wants us to.'

On 17th September their daughter was born. They named her Lydia.

'The cholera seems to be losing its grip on Bristol,' Craik said, three weeks later.

'It's true,' Müller agreed. 'Last night the funeral bell rang only once.'

'And it's been quiet so far this morning.'

'I think we should have a day of thanksgiving,' suggested Henry. 'Although so many have died, many thousands more haven't. We've a lot to be thankful for.'

George thought of baby Lydia, well and content at home with his wife.

'That's a splendid idea,' he said.

'God has even used the cholera to make people think about where they would go if they died,' Craik went on.

Müller shook his head. 'But it's so sad that it took that to bring them to their senses.'

'It doesn't matter why they came,' his friend reminded him. 'The strangers who turned up at the service on Sunday and who stayed behind to pray seemed to be genuine in their search for the Lord.'

'Yes,' agreed George. 'God used even the cholera to show them he loved them.'

Müller kept his journal faithfully.

'May 29th 1833 Review of the last twelve months, since we have been in Bristol ... Bethesda, ... increased to 60 in number, and 49 more have come to Gideon church; that's an increase, within the year, of 109.'

'June 12th I felt, this morning, that we might do something for the souls of those poor boys and girls, and adult or aged people, to whom we have given bread every day for some time, by establishing a school for them, reading the Scriptures to them, and speaking to them about the Lord.'

'We have prayed about it, now I think we must act.' It was Craik who spoke.

George agreed. 'It does seem that the Lord is leading us to found The Scripture Knowledge Institution.'

'Let's work this out in detail,' Craik's chair scraped the floor as he pulled it in to his desk. 'What are our objectives?'

After a minute's thought Müller replied, 'One. To help Day Schools, Sunday Schools and Adult Schools, in which teaching is based on scriptural principles, and, as far as the Lord gives the funds, and supplies us with suitable teachers, and in other ways shows us his will, to open schools of this kind.'

Craik smiled. 'I couldn't have put it better myself!'

'Two.' George went on, 'To distribute the Holy Scriptures.'

'And three,' Craik spoke as he wrote, 'to help missionary efforts.' He dried the nib of his pen and placed it in its holder. 'And may God bless all we do for him.'

In the spring of 1834 Müller sat at his desk.

He turned back to the previous page of his journal and read, 'March 19th, evening. When I got home after preaching at Bethesda, I heard the joyful news that my dear wife had been delivered at twenty minutes past eight of a little boy.'

George smiled as he thought of his baby son, Elijah.

Picking up his pen, he dipped it in the ink, and wrote.

'April 14th. The Craiks and ourselves have been living together till now but as the Lord has given them one child, and to us two we have come at last to the conclusion that it would be better if we lived in separate houses.'

Soon settled in their respective homes, the Craiks and Müllers continued their work together.

'I am so looking forward to seeing my dear brother again,' Mary said, looking out the window for the twentieth time in an hour. She sat down, lifting Lydia up on to her knee. 'You'll see your uncle soon, my dear, and he will meet his little niece and nephew. Uncle Anthony has come all the way from Persia.'

There was much hugging and laughing,

much singing and praying over the next few days, as Mary and her brother caught up with each other's doings.

'Have you decided?' Anthony Groves asked George, 'Will you come with me?'

'Yes,' Müller replied, 'I'll come with you. It'll be strange to be back in Europe. But if I can help you interview missionary candidates, and see my father and brother, it will be a worthwhile trip.'

'You may be able to speak to them about the Lord.' It was Mary who spoke.

'Pray God they will listen,' George said softly.

It was a very different George Müller who arrived at Heimersleben in April 1835 from the young drunk who had once caused such havoc and unhappiness there.

'He looks so old,' he thought, as he kissed his father on both cheeks.

Herr Müller held his son at arms' length. 'You are thinner than you were. Is it well with you?'

The two men sat down, one on either side of the fire.

'It's very well with me, Father. God has been good.'

They talked in the light of the dying sun, George telling his father about Mary and the children, about Bristol and the cholera outbreak there.

'And are you adequately paid for the work you do?' Herr Müller asked.

George swallowed hard. 'Even in his old age, ' he thought, 'his mind is on money.' But the instant he had thought the thought, he felt sorry for it. His father was not asking how much he had in the bank, he was asking if he had enough to live on.

'Father, I have things to tell you that you'll hardly believe.'

They spoke long into the night, George telling of sovereigns given here, legs of mutton there.

'And you are telling me,' Herr Müller said, when only the dying embers of the fire lit the room, ' that Craik and you run two boys' schools, three girls' schools and educate adults as well, all on no regular income?'

'And that's only the half of it,' his son concluded.

When George left a few days later, his father had a great deal to think about.

Stopping for the night in Celle, en route back to England, George wrote his journal.

'April 9th Yesterday morning I drove with my father to Halbertstadt, where we said a tearful goodbye. ... I found myself again on the road to Brunswick, which I had travelled twice in the service of the devil, and now I was travelling in the name of Jesus. It was a strange feeling, passing the inn at Wolfenbüttel, the same place where I'd run from the innkeeper right into the arms of the law!'

———

'If the Lord
wills, we will.'

———

Bristol's street children

'It seems as though Father's near his end,' Mary spoke softly.

George held her close.

'And when he goes, my dear, he will hear his Heavenly Father's "Well done."'

'I have no doubt about that,' Mary agreed, 'but I will miss him such a lot.' She looked at the two children asleep in their cots. 'And they won't even remember him.'

It was no surprise when, the next morning, Mr Groves died.

'They are both very unwell,' the doctor said, looking at Lydia and Elijah the following day. 'He has inflammation of the chest, and will need very careful nursing. It will come to a crisis, and if he comes through that ... '

Mary sat down heavily in the chair between their cots.

'My father ... my children .... '

George put his arms around his wife, tears glinting in his eyes, 'They are safe in the arms of Jesus,' he assured her. 'He loves them even more than we do.'

There was little sleep in the Müller house that night. Tiny foreheads were mopped, prayers poured out from aching hearts, and words of comfort filled the sickroom. George sang in a soft voice, as he cradled Lydia. Mary stroked Elijah's face, and spoke words of love to him. All of the next day the sick children were nursed with the tenderest of care and by evening Lydia seemed just a little bit better. Her baby brother was not.

'Dear Lord, help us through this terrible time,' George prayed. 'And if you are going to take Elijah, take him soon, Father. Spare the dear child from suffering.'

Two hours later baby Elijah was called from his home on earth to his home in heaven and, on the day of the funeral, 29th June 1835, grandfather and infant grandson were placed in the same grave.

♦ ♦ ♦

'There are destitute children on every street corner,' George told his wife. 'The youngest of them beg, and the older ones get money however they can.'

'I've heard that pickpockets are everywhere, some as young as seven or eight.'

'That's true. And many of them are put there by rogues who take what the children steal and leave them no better off.'

'Why are there so many street children?'

'There always have been some,' George said,

'but a lot of those out there now were orphaned by the cholera.'

Mary looked at Lydia, warm and well-dressed. 'Is there nothing we can do for them?'

George stood up. 'I believe there is. It has been on my mind for some time. Think of it, Mary, an orphanage to house them and give them a Christian upbringing, a place where they would be safe, fed, clothed and educated. If God were to do all that without any appeals for money, any fund-raising, any begging .. what an impact that would make on unbelievers and weak Christians alike.'

Mary watched her husband pace up and down their sitting-room. 'Where would you begin?'

'I've already begun in the one way that matters,' he assured her. 'I've been praying about it.'

Looking down at Lydia, playing in front of the fire with a peg doll, he saw in his mind's eye other girls her age. The streets were their home, their agility and wit kept them fed, and they were heading for lives of poverty, crime ... or worse.

Müller dipped his pen in the ink, thought for a moment, then wrote. '2nd December, 1835 Today I took the first step towards opening a home for orphan girls. I've had leaflets printed announcing a public meeting on December 9th at which I intend to tell people my thinking.'

'What is in the parcel?' he asked his wife a few weeks later.

She unwrapped it, 'Five knives, five forks, six dessert spoons and twelve teaspoons, all for the Orphan House.'

'Have you the list of what has been given so far?'

'It's never far from me,' Mary laughed, 'because it's in constant use.'

He sat down. 'Read it to me, please. On the last day of the year, I want to count my blessings!'

Mary took a deep breath. 'One couple willing to work without pay, and donating the furniture and contents of their home. One woman, also wishes to work for nothing.' Then, in a sing song voice, she went on, 'six dishes, thirty plates, four basins, one jug, four mugs, three salt stands, three graters, four knives, five forks, one blanket, twenty nine yards of cloth, one counterpane, eight cups and saucers, one flat iron stand, one sugar basin, four combs.' She stopped for breath, 'and the contents of the parcel on my knee.'

'Plus £154 in cash, George added. 'And all without asking anyone for anything.'

It was a list of a different kind that Mary read the following April. 'Christina Walker, Daisy Black, Jane Mason, Eliza Baxter and Lottie Farms. How many applications have been made?'

'Twenty-six, including these ones,' her husband answered.

'I thought there were more than that.'

'More, yes,' he agreed. 'But twenty-six were within our age limits. We can't take them if they are under seven or over twelve.'

Mary looked distressed. 'And what happens to six year olds or four year olds? We could have sisters separated, one taken in and one left out.'

'We have thirty places in No 6 Wilson Street and twenty-six children. But as soon as the doors are open more applications will come in. We can't fill it up with infants,' George said.

'But could we not open a home especially for the little ones?' his wife asked.

'If the Lord wills, we will.'

A thrill ran up Mary's spine. How often she had heard him say that. And how often God had done what seemed to be impossible.

Six months later George recorded in his journal, 'October 19th 1836 Today, after having prayed about it for a long time, I've taken on a lady as matron for the Infants' Orphan House. Although there has been enough money to do it before now, this is the first really suitable person we've met. There have also been applications on behalf of several orphaned infants.'

Six days later, he wrote, 'Today we obtained very suitable premises for the Infants' House. How good God is! If we'd spent a fortune building a house we'd hardly have been able to improve on the one we've got. It's number 1 Wilson Street, just along the road from the girls' house at number 6. God's hand is obviously in this. It is so important to leave all our cares with him, the big ones and the small ones too, because he arranges things so perfectly.'

'What is the programme for tomorrow?'

Mary asked. Her husband looked up from his papers, sat back in his chair, and relaxed.

'It is to be a whole day of prayer and thanksgiving for the Infants' House. And what a lot we have to be thankful for! All that was needed was given, and not a penny was asked for. And it is now home to our four to six year old orphans.'

'Do you remember what you said on the last day of last year?' Mary asked.

He looked puzzled.

'You said, regarding the Orphan House, "If the Lord wills, we will".'

George smiled. 'And he did. And we have. And all in less than eleven months!'

The following night Müller wrote in his journal, 'This day was set apart for prayer and thanksgiving for the Infants' House, which was opened on November 28th. In the morning we had a prayer meeting. In the afternoon, as well as prayer and thanksgiving, I addressed the children of our day schools and the orphans, about 350 of them.'

On 2nd December 1835, George had prayed that God would provide £1000 for his work with orphans. By 15th June 1837 every penny of that had been given.

'The orphanages received their first legacy today,' George told Mary, as they sat at their evening meal.

'Do we know who left it to the work?'

' I'll tell you as much as I know,' he said, laying down his knife and fork. 'This morning we

received a parcel with clothes and some money.'
Among the donations in money there was an
envelope separate from the rest containing the
legacy of six shillings and sixpence halfpenny, from
a dear boy, a Christian, who had died.'

Mary forgot the food in front of her as she
listened. Having lost a little boy of her own, she
was particularly caught by the story.

'During his last illness some money was given
to the child in gifts. Shortly before he fell asleep
for the last time, he requested that his treasure
might be sent to the orphans.'

'It may only be a small amount,' Mary said,
'but will any other legacy ever be worth so much?'

'Object to a boys' home! I can't believe
people feel like that!' Müller said to his assistant
some days later. 'You would think that they would
be happier to have a boys' orphan home in their
street rather than a gang of pickpockets and
beggars.'

'But I'm afraid they do. We must rethink
where to open our third home. The people living
beside the house you've rented are threatening
the landlord because he has let it to a charity.'

Müller shook his head. 'May God forgive
them.' After a few minutes' thought, he asked,
'Could it be that it is not God's will that we open
another home?'

There was a knock at the door, and an
envelope was handed it. Opening it, Müller's
assistant found it contained £50 for furniture for
the boys' orphan house.

'I think I have in my hand the answer to your question.'

'I think you do,' Müller agreed. 'But where is it going to be?'

Some weeks later a third large house became vacant on the very same street as the other two. It was immediately rented to be used as a boys' orphan home.

Müller worked hard, very hard. He was not strong, and often suffered illness. So weak was he at the end of November 1837, that he thought he might not recover. He wrote in his journal, 'I have written to my father; perhaps for the last time. All is well, all will be well, all cannot but be well, because I am in Christ. How precious that I don't have to struggle to find the Lord now that I'm ill, for I know him as my Saviour already.'

Some weeks later, still not recovered enough to go out, George looked from his room window just as a long line of orphan girls threaded their way down Wilson Street on their way to church.

'There's Mr Müller at the window,' Eliza whispered.

'Where?'

Eliza nodded in the direction of the window, it not being ladylike to point.

'He looks so pale and thin,' Lottie sounded worried, 'some say he's going to die. Do you think he will?'

'No,' Eliza said firmly. 'I nearly died once, of the cholera, and I was thinner and paler than Mr Müller. But I got better again'

Lottie immediately found something else to worry about. 'I'm scared the cholera will come back again.'

'Did you catch it too?' Eliza whispered.

They were not meant to talk as they walked two by two along the road, and Miss Fletcher was watching.

'No, but my mother did, and she died of it. That's why I came to the orphanage.'

'Did your Father die of it too?'

'I can't remember him,' her friend explained. 'He was killed in an accident when they started building the bridge over the Avon Gorge.'

'Was that why they stopped?' Eliza was always full of questions.

'Shhh!' Miss Fletcher had caught Lottie's eye. She would have to wait until they were back in the orphan home to tell her friend that the bridge building was stopped because they had run out of money.

'This morning,' George told Mary later, 'I saw thirty-two orphan girls pass under my window on their way to the chapel. When I looked at these dear children in their clean dresses, and their comfortable warm cloaks, walking nicely under the care of a sister, I felt so grateful to God that he had used us to help provide for them.'

'They are cosy and clean instead of being ragged and dirty,' Lydia said, tiptoeing to look out the window.

'They've gone, I'm afraid. They'll be eating their soup by now.'

'Instead of being poor and hungry,' added Lydia.

Her father took her on his knee. 'But more important than their dresses and cloaks, and even more important than their bowls of soup on a cold day like this, is that they are learning about the Lord Jesus, and what he has done for them.'

It was Müller's habit to take stock of each year when it came to its end. On 31st December 1837 he wrote, 'There are now 81 children in the three Orphan Houses, and nine Christian brothers and sisters who care for them. Ninety, therefore, daily sit down to table. The schools need even more help than before, particularly the Sunday School, in which there are at present about 320 children. Around 350 are in the day schools.'

George Müller

'To assist Day Schools, Sunday Schools and Adult Schools. To circulate the Holy Scriptures. And to aid missionary efforts.'

Pennies from heaven

'Dad,' said nine-year-old Lydia, 'you're very good at counting.'

George looked up from the page of figures on which he was working.

'I wish I could count long sums like that,' she went on, 'then I could help you.'

'That time will come,' her father said.
'Who taught you how to keep accounts, Dad? Did you learn at school?'

Müller sat back in his chair and looked at the girl. 'I think it is time you found out something about your father,' he said. 'Sit down by the fire and I'll tell you a story ... a true story of a boy just your age and how he learned to keep accounts.'

'... so you see, my dear, by the time I was nine years old I was very good at counting money, but not very good at telling the truth.'

Lydia sat listening to every word. 'I don't think I want to know about you stealing the money and hiding it in your shoe,' she said quietly. 'I want to forget that.'

'That's because you love me,' her father went on. 'And God understands how you feel. You see

God loves me even more than you do, enough to forgive me for all the wicked things I've done, even for stealing my father's money.'

'Are you sure,' the girl asked, 'quite sure that God has forgiven you?'

George knelt down in front of his daughter's chair.

'I know I'm forgiven,' he assured her. 'The Bible tells me that those who confess their sins have them washed away, and that God doesn't even remember them.'

He went to his desk and picked up his account book. 'And the wonderful thing is that God trusts me to look after all this money for him, enough to feed hundreds of hungry children.'

Lydia's face broke into a broad smile. 'Then God really must have forgiven you.'

She sounded relieved. Müller settled down to his accounts. After watching the flames dancing in the fire for some time, Lydia looked up.

'Dad, she said, 'Does God always give you enough money to feed all the children?'

'Yes,' Müller answered without looking up.

'You must have hundreds of pounds in the bank then.'

Her father beckoned her to his desk.

'Sit down and I'll tell you two more true stories,' he told her.

She looked apprehensive. 'Will I want to forget them afterwards?' she asked.

Müller laughed. 'No, my pretty one, you'll want to remember them all of your life.'

'Look here,' he said, pointing to figures for a day the previous week. 'Just before I left to go to the prayer meeting that day something that was given to the homes was sold for £2 2s. But I knew that wasn't quite enough for all we needed to buy.'

'What happened,' Lydia asked, 'did the children not get enough to eat?'

'Well, what happened was this. The Infant Orphans' teacher took the little ones for a walk late that morning. As they were going up the street a poor woman approached her, and gave her two pence to be spent on whatever the orphans needed. "It is not much," she told the teacher, "but I must give it to you." When I came home from the meeting I needed one penny more than the £2 2s to pay the baker for bread. But before I had begun to wonder where I would get the penny from, the teacher handed me the old woman's two pence.'

'So you were able to buy the bread and you still had a penny left over,' the girl added. 'What's the other story? You said you'd tell me two.'

Her father pointed to the last set of figures in the book.

'Yesterday,' he told her, 'I knew we required a lot of shillings for the Boys' Orphan House. I had some money left over from the day before, but was eight pence short. However we found we had another seven pence to hand.'

'So you only needed one more penny. Did you get it?'

'Listen,' he smiled at her impatience. 'Listen and I'll tell you. One of our helpers heard that an elderly lady had put some money into the box in the Girls' Orphan Home. So he went there, opened the box, and found that what had been put in was a one penny piece, just exactly what we needed. And the boys were able to have their lunch yesterday. They have never once gone without.'

'Does that mean you have no money at all for today?' Lydia asked.

Müller laughed. I haven't finished yesterday's story yet. 'After the things for lunch were bought a lady, a minister's wife, sent us half a sovereign for the orphan work. That was kept towards today's needs. And already this morning seventeen shillings has come in from the sale of stockings and other items. So we are well on our way to feeding them all today.'

'I've a story to tell you both,' George said as he sat down with Mary and Lydia at the dinner table a few months later.

Mary smiled. She knew there was no point in serving the meal until the tale had been told. The food would just get cold.

'I'm not going to tell you the name of the man involved, just what he did,' Müller explained, knowing that the guest who had stayed with them for the past few days would not want Mary and Lydia to know what he had done in private.

Lydia listened eagerly.

'There was a man,' her father went on, ' who

had a piece of land. He divided the land into sections, and decided that what grew in one of the sections would be for the orphans. He prayed over the land, asking God to give a good crop. He and his family continued to pray over it throughout the growing season. Well, God answered their prayers and the land gave a good crop of potatoes.'

''Did he bring them in bags to the Orphan House?' the girl asked.

'Shhh...' Mary said, 'let Dad finish.'

George went on. 'Because he stays some distance away the man sold the potatoes and brought the money he got for them, two whole sovereigns.'

'God is so good,' Mary said.

'And it's exciting!' added Lydia.

But there were things of which even Mary knew nothing. In March 1844 one of the Orphan House workers was approached by a lady who lived with her father in the street in which all three homes were situated.

'My father and I wish to give up the rent of our house,' she explained, 'and to move elsewhere. I'm sure Mr Müller has no intention of opening a fourth home on the street, but, if he has......'

When George heard of the house his mind started working overtime.

'What are the points in favour of opening another house?' he asked himself. 'One. There are more applications than places in our present houses. Two. If we were to open a further home, it would make good sense for it to be alongside the other ones in Wilson Street. Three. There are about fifteen children in the Infant House who are too old to be there, but for whom there is no other place. Four. I know of two ladies who would work in a new home. Five. There is £300 to hand at present. And six, it would be proof of the Lord's blessing on the way we depend on him for our every need, and an encouragement to others to do the same.'

Müller sat back in his chair. 'I'll say nothing to anyone, not even Mary, and say everything to the Lord.'

Twenty-two days later, having prayed earnestly over that time, Müller visited the lady and her father.

'I really am so sorry,' the father said, after they had talked together for some time. 'As we had not heard from you we assumed that you were not interested. Consequently, we rethought our plans and have decided to remain here ourselves.'

Bidding them a friendly goodbye, he left the house, having been asked to call back in a week.

But he did not stop praying.

'My dear Sir,' the father greeted him warmly on his next visit. 'The very day you were last here I went out and found a most suitable house for my daughter and myself. We have decided to move after all. This house is yours to rent if that can be arranged with its owner.'

And it was. June was spent preparing the

house, and in July the first orphans moved in.

'Am I old enough to help you, Dad?' Lydia asked. 'You have so much to do.'

Müller thought for a minute. Then, remembering how his childhood efforts at accounting had been used by way of preparation for his life's work, he agreed.

'You will have to explain what the different books are for.'

'Yes, I will do that. But I think we could create a job for you that would relieve both your mother and myself.'

Lydia was pleased.

'Start by telling me why you have so many different books.'

George pulled open the bottom right-hand drawer of his desk and took out a set of ledgers.

The next hour seemed to pass in ten minutes.

'But I thought all the money you were given went to the orphans.'

'No,' her father smiled at her surprise, 'there are many other parts to our work.'

He opened the big thirteen-paned glass door of the bookcase that sat opposite his desk. Taking out a sheaf of papers, he found the one he wanted and handed it to his daughter. 'Here you have it as Brother Craik and I worked it out years ago. Nothing much has changed.'

Lydia read aloud. 'To assist Day Schools, Sunday Schools and Adult Schools. To circulate the Holy Scriptures. And to aid missionary efforts.'

Handing the sheet back to her father, she

asked, 'And all of that is paid for without asking anyone for money?'

'That's right,' he agreed. 'If money comes in earmarked for a specific thing, for example, the orphans, it goes to that cause. If we are free to choose how it is spent, we allocate it between the different causes.'

'And there has always been enough for everything that needed to be done?' she queried.

'There have been times when I have only had a farthing to meet all our needs. But there has never been a time when I only had a farthing and had to pay a halfpenny.'

'What's the job I can do for you?' asked Lydia.

Mr Müller took a hard-backed notebook from his desk drawer. 'Have a look at this,' he said.

She took it over to the window, stretched out on her father's couch, and read.

Gift	silver chain
Date Received	26th May 1843
Date Sold	27th May 1843
Selling price	1s

Gift	lady's boots (worn)
Date Received	2nd June 1843
Date Sold	3rd June 1843
Selling Price	1s 4d

Gift	silver pencil case (broken)
Date Received	7th June 1843
Date Sold	7th June 1843
Selling Price	6d

George Müller

Gift	*gentleman's cloak*
Date Received	7th June 1843
Date sold	11th June 1843
Selling Price	4s

She flicked through the pages. 'Are these all the gifts you are given to sell?'

'Yes,' her father said. 'That's exactly what they are. Would you like to take over keeping that book?'

Lydia thought of her mother, and of how pale she sometimes looked.

'Yes,' she said. 'I'd like to do that. And perhaps one day I'll be as good at keeping books as you are.'

Her father laughed. 'Or better!'

'When can I start?' the girl asked.

'As soon as you have unwrapped that parcel under the window,' Müller said, pointing to a large brown paper package. And remember, fold the paper carefully and wind up the string ready to use again.'

Lydia looked at her father. 'Do you ever waste anything?' she teased.

'This evening I received £1,000 towards the Building Fund. When I opened this donation I was as calm, as perfectly calm as if I had received a single penny, because, by God's grace, I have faith in him, and therefore am looking for answers to my prayers, and am sure that God will give every shilling that is needed.'

George Müller on answered prayer

Ashley Down

'Have you read this letter?' Müller asked, handing it to Henry Craik.

His friend sat down, unfolded the sheet of paper, noted the date: 30th October 1845, and read it through twice. 'There is perhaps some truth in it,' he said thoughtfully.

'I'm sure there is,' replied Müller, 'and the tone of the letter shows no ill will. How does he put it?'

Craik read, 'The inhabitants of some of the houses adjoining the Orphan Houses are, in various ways, inconvenienced by their being in Wilson Street.'

There was a long silence, both men being deep in thought.

'Let's talk this over,' Müller suggested.

'After we've prayed it through,' agreed Craik, lowering himself to his knees.

That evening as they ate their meal, Müller told Mary and Lydia the main points of his discussion with Craik.

'There must be a lot of noise at times,' he said.

'Especially during the play-hours when the children are outside,' agreed Lydia.

'I'm only sorry I hadn't thought of that before,' George sounded rather sad, 'I've been asking other people to put up with noise I should find tiresome.'

'What else did you discuss?' Mary asked.

'There is the matter of the drains. Because of the number of children in the houses, several times the drains have choked, affecting the water to the neighbours' houses.'

Lydia pulled a face.

'And the children have no proper playgrounds in Wilson Street. The one there is only just large enough for the children from one house at a time.'

'Does that matter?' his daughter asked.

'Yes, I think it does. Some of the children have brothers and sisters in other houses, and under the present system they never play together.'

All three considered the situation.

'Apart from these disadvantages of Wilson Street, there would be some real benefits in moving,' George went on.

'The children could have gardens to play in,' Lydia said.

'And to work in, places where the older boys could learn to grow things. They could produce potatoes and vegetables for the Orphan Houses. That would reduce our costs, and the food would be fresher too.'

Lydia looked excited. 'They could keep hens too, and rear chickens ... and ducklings ... and..'

Mary laughed. 'Your father is a pastor, not a farmer.'

But George looked thoughtful.

'Working outside would be so much better for the older boys,' his wife agreed. 'It distresses me to see them cooped up in the Houses knitting their socks. And the fresh air would be so good for them. Some of them are puny little creatures.'

'They would have a better chance of health if they could enjoy bracing fresh air.'

'Yes,' Mary agreed. 'I can see that spacious houses in a less built up area would be good for the children.'

'It would benefit the staff too,' George thought aloud. 'They would have more space, greater freedom and a degree of privacy.'

And his ever practical wife added, 'Think of it. The laundry could be done on the premises, not sent out to washerwomen. That would give the older girls work to do, work that would train them for going into service when they leave the homes.'

'But where will you find houses for all the orphan children?' asked Lydia.

'That I don't know,' her father answered.

'The Lord will provide the money,' Lydia said firmly.

George looked at his daughter. 'If the Lord wills, we will.'

'How often I've heard him say that,' Mary thought to herself, 'and it usually heralds something big.'

A week later George and Mary discussed the matter again.

'There are no suitable premises for sale in Bristol,' he said. 'I feel the Lord is leading us to build our own.'

Mary thought about that. 'How many would you aim to accommodate?'

The reply came quickly. 'Three hundred orphans, along with their teachers, helpers and servants. The number of applications for admission is greater now than it ever has been.'

'Will you discuss it with the leaders in church at the meeting tonight?'

'That's my intention,' he said. 'And we'll take it from there.'

Mary waited up for his return. From the spring in his step as he mounted the stairs, she knew the outcome of the meeting before her husband came in the door.

'Unanimous,' he said. 'Everyone agreed that we ought to leave Wilson Street, and none saw reasons against building.'

'I think we need to be up a little earlier in the morning,' he said as they went to bed, 'We have a lot of work to do. We have to pray this project through.'

Müller's early training in accounting was called into use yet again. 'I've calculated that to buy land somewhere in the neighbourhood of Bristol, build premises and furnish them would cost more than £10,000,' he told Mary one morning as they knelt to pray.

'Remember what you said,' she said. 'If the Lord wills, we will.'

His reply was firm. 'Of that I have no doubt ... no doubt at all.'

Fifteen days of earnest prayer later, not a single penny had been given for the building of a new orphan house.

Sitting in his study in December 1845, Müller reviewed the closing year. Picking up his pen, he dipped it in the inkwell, and wrote his journal.

'God is more than able to move people to help finance the building of this house if it is his will.... After family prayer in the morning I had my usual time for prayer about the building, and I was particularly full of thanksgiving for the £50 received yesterday evening, and felt a real burden of prayer for the person who gave it. I was now looking out for more, as I am doing day by day, when this afternoon a person from Clevedon donated 2s 6d, her grandson sent 6d with it, and from the Christian lady who brought the money, the gift of a further 6d. These donations, though small, are nevertheless very precious to me, as I take them as further proof from God, that he is blessing this project and that he'll finish the work he has started. This evening I received £1,000 towards the Building Fund. When I opened this donation I was as calm, as perfectly calm as if I had received a single penny, because, by God's grace, I have faith in him, and therefore am looking for answers to my prayers, and am sure that God will give every shilling that is needed.'

'I heard of a possible piece of land,' Müller told Craik. 'It's out of the city, at Ashley Down.'

'Is it big enough for our needs?' his friend asked.

'Yes. There's seven acres.'

Craik was interested. 'And the price?'

'£1400. £200 per acre.'

'Will you go to see it?' Craik asked.

'I'll go this evening,' Müller said.

'The land looks ideal,' he told Mary later that night. 'It's big, reasonably flat, just right for our purpose.

'And the seller?'

'He wasn't at home.'

'Will you go back later?'

'I don't think so. I'll wait a day or two. His servant will tell him I called.

'God is so good!' Müller announced, as he walked into Craik's study a day or two later.

Henry closed his book. 'You've been back to Ashley Down?'

'I have,' agreed George, pulling a chair up to his friend's desk. 'And the Lord had been before me. I saw the owner and he told me this story. He awoke at three o'clock this morning and didn't get back to sleep till five. While he was lying awake, his mind was active on the subject of the piece of land that was for sale, and in which the Orphan House had shown an interest. By the time five o'clock in the morning came round, he had decided that should we offer to buy the land he would sell it to us for £120 per acre rather than £200. We have to let him know our thinking.'

Without another word the two men slipped to their knees and prayed fervently for God's guidance. Before the morning was over the land was theirs!

Three days later Müller wrote inviting an architect to look at the land. His reply, by return of post, read:

'My dear Sir, it will give me the greatest pleasure, more than I can possibly express in a letter, to lend you a helping hand in the wonderful work of love in which you are involved. I will count it the greatest privilege to be allowed to use my training as an architect and surveyor in the erection of the home that is to be built for the orphans. I really do mean what I say, and, if all is well, by the blessing of God, I will let you have the plans, elevations and sections, with all the necessary specifications required for the costing of the work. And all this will be done gratuitously. I will also forego any payment for the estimates and for the work involved in superintending the building work.'

That evening Mary read the letter then handed it to Lydia.

'Does gratuitously mean he will do it without charge?' the girl asked.

'Quite right,' her father told her, 'he will do it as a gift for the children and a love gift for the Lord.'

'Will you start building right away?'

'No, Lydia,' George explained. 'We'll start

building when we have all the money we need, not before.'

Müller turned back the pages of his journal and read the pages with pleasure. 'February 28th 1846 Today £500 was promised.' 'July 6th Today I was given the sum of £2050, of which £2000 is for the Building Fund. A further 2s 6d also came in.' 'July 10th Received £120, of which £100 is intended by the donor for the Building Fund.' 'October 18th Today the Lord has greatly refreshed my heart by sending £120.' 'October 29th This morning I had been again bringing the case of the building before the Lord in prayer, begging him to have things move along quickly if that was his will, and *the very instant I rose from my knees*, I was handed a letter with a money order for £300.' 'November 14th Since this day last year God has given me, in answer to prayer, a most suitable piece of ground, and £6.304 for the Building Fund, and about £2,700 for present use for the work.'

Kneeling beside his couch, George bowed his head. 'Dear Lord,' he prayed, 'please bless the work we're involved in on behalf of the orphans. If it is your will, move people to give the money sooner rather than later so that the work might be done quickly.'

He rose to his feet, settled back down to his work, but was interrupted within the hour.

'This came for you,' Mary said, ' handing him a package.'

She watched as he opened it. Together they

enjoyed and rejoiced in the gift it contained, a gift of £2000.

As the months passed God continued to answer their prayers.

Sitting in his study by the light of the setting summer sun Müller wrote, 'June 23rd This day the Lord, in his great goodness, encouraged us with a large donation to the Building Fund. Such gifts encourage me more than I can say.'

It was a lovely evening on 5th July 1847, an evening Lydia would never forget, when her father announced that every penny that was needed had been given. The work of building the Orphan Home at Ashley Down had begun.

They didn't rise from the table immediately after dinner. Instead, they sat for some time praying, singing verses of hymns, and enjoying the certainty that God was at work, that God was doing great things.

'I remember what you said when we first talked about moving from Wilson Street,' Lydia told her father.

He looked puzzled.

Mary smiled. 'So do I.'

'What was that?' George asked.

The two women in his life said it together. 'If the Lord wills, we will.'

Müller's soft eyes shone, with gratitude and perhaps with tears. 'And the Lord has willed in a most wonderful way,' he said. 'Most wonderful.'

Lydia and her father talked on after Mary went to bed.

'I sometimes think back to my childhood in Prussia,' he told his daughter. 'By the time I was your age I was a thief and a liar. I had done unspeakable things and had even been in prison.'

Mary listened. Her father's past no longer upset her, knowing as she did that he was forgiven, that he was a new creation through Jesus Christ.

'And it seems to me a strange providence that the Lord should choose me to gather in these funds for him, thousands and thousands of pounds over the years. It is almost as though, with each donation however small, he is reminding me that I'm not now who I was then. I'm no longer a playboy in Prussia, I'm an ambassador for King Jesus.'

'Does that make me an ambassador's daughter?' Lydia asked.

Müller look into the eyes of his only surviving child and, knowing her to be a Christian, he replied with assurance. 'Better than that, my dear, you're a princess. You're a daughter of the King of Kings.'

Picking up his Bible before going to bed that night, George took from it a folded sheet of paper. He opened it and read the letter Lydia had written some time before. Reading it thrilled his heart.

'My very dear Father and Mother,

I am so glad that you are better. I was glad to get dear mother's kind note. Dearest Father and Mother, I wished to tell you that I was now happy, but I have not liked to, and I thought I could better tell you in writing than by speaking. I do not know exactly the time when I first was happy in the prospect of death and eternity, but I know that the work of God in my heart was very gradual. I can now say *Thanks be unto God for his unspeakable gift*. Please dear Father and Mother, continue to pray for me, that I may be kept from dishonouring God, and that I may be more and more thankful to him for the gift of his Son, and for my dear parents, my dear Aunty, my dear teachers, and all kind friends who love me and pray for me. And now, dear Father and Mother, with much love,

I remain your affectionate little daughter,
Lydia Müller

'My princess,' George thought, replacing the letter in his Bible.

'Have you asked God for the gift of faith?'
'Is your God able to answer all requests?'
'I don't believe that he has ever refused to give anyone who asked for it the gift of faith.'
George Müller's talks about faith with a would-be benefactor.

No boxes big enough

'How long will it be before the new Orphan House will be finished, Mr Müller?' Anna asked one day in February 1849, when he visited the girls' home in which she had lived for four years.

'I think, he replied, 'that it will be ready in about six weeks' time.'

'May I ask another question?' she asked shyly.

George nodded.

'How long has it taken to gather the money to build the fine new home?'

'I can tell you that exactly,' he told her,' because I mark it off in my diary. I started to pray for the money needed for the building one thousand, one hundred and ninety-five days ago.'

Anna's eyes opened wide.

'But that is forever, sir.'

'Not quite, Müller told her. 'Let's work it out. How many days are in a week?'

'Seven, sir,' she replied.

If we divide that great number of days by seven we find that it is one hundred and seventy weeks and five days.

'That is a lot of weeks, sir,' Anna said.

'And how many weeks are in a year?' he asked her.

'Sir, there are fifty two.'

'If we divide the weeks by fifty-two, we discover that in three years, fourteen weeks and five days the Lord has provided for the building of the New Orphan Home. How good he is.'

Anna collected all her courage together. 'Could God not have given it in one day?' she dared to ask.

Müller looked deep into her eyes. There was no cheekiness there, just puzzlement.

'Can you think why he might not?' he asked the child.

Anna thought for a moment. 'I suppose that there would not be a box big enough to hold it all,' she decided.

'I'm sure there would not,' he agreed. 'Nor would we have known what to do with it.'

Satisfied, Anna went back to her friends.

'Lord,' Müller prayed silently as he strode back home,' how often I would have asked you to give all we needed right away. Thank you for not doing that, but satisfying our needs a day at a time, and for giving us time to plan the new home properly.' He smiled as he prayed, 'Thank you, Father, that there was not a box big enough to take £15,784 18s 10d all at once.'

'Look at that!' William said to his friend as they walked two by two from their old home in Wilson Street to Ashley Down on 19th March, 1849.

Miss Taylor overheard them. 'That, boys, is your new home,' she explained.

The crocodile of boys stopped, open-mouthed and wide-eyed.

'Let's have an arithmetic puzzle,' she suggested. 'How many windows can you see?'

Archibald Mason's hand was first in the air. Miss Taylor nodded in his direction.

'I can see forty-eight altogether,' he said, 'eighteen on the first and second floors, eleven on the third and one high up on the tower.'

'That's quite right,' she agreed, 'and there are many more in the back.'

'The inside must be as light as the outside,' William decided.

Looking at him Miss Taylor remembered the day she had collected William from his own home. His grandmother, who had cared from him and his brothers after their parents died of cholera, could cope no longer in her single room, up a dark and damp close. Little light had penetrated through the tiny window and the candle which fought against the draught to stay lit had given so little light that it only seemed to make the room seem even darker than it was.

'Yes, William,' she agreed. 'Even in winter the Orphan House will be as light as any house in Bristol.'

'I like it when the sun shines into a room,' the boy told her.

'I'm sure you do,' she thought. 'And I quite understand why.'

The girls moved to their new home two days later. Anna and Isabella were at the front of the long line as usual.

'What does it look like?' Anna asked Miss Fletcher, who walked alongside her.

'It is very beautiful,' her teacher told her.

Isabella's excitement got the better of her. 'Please, Ma'am,' she asked, 'Please tell us about it.'

Anna was puzzled by Miss Fletcher's expression. Normally she looked quite serious. Today the lines on her face seemed softer. The girl had never before noticed how blue her teacher's eyes were.

'No,' she said, but not crossly, 'wait and see it for yourselves.'

'I think it will be six storeys high,' Anna said to Isabella.

'Wrong,' said Miss Fletcher.

'I think it will be five storeys high,' Isabella guessed.

Miss Archer laughed, 'Wrong again.'

'She playing a game!' Anna realised. 'Miss Fletcher's playing a game.' Now this was fun and she had to make the most of it.

The girls behind saw what was happening and listened.

By the time they reached Ashley Down the news had rippled back along the line to the very last girl that the New Orphan Home was two storeys high in some places and three in others. There was a tower in the middle of it and a door with pillars at each side. It was bigger and brighter and more beautiful than any of the grand houses in the city of Bristol. In front of the home was a large circle in which bushes and trees and flowers had been planted.

But none of their accumulated knowledge prepared the girls for their first sight of their new home. Even Anna was silent as she took it in.

'Isabella,' she said, after her first long look. 'Mr Müller said that God gave the money to build the new Home in eleven hundred and ninety-five days.'

'Why did it take so long?' her friend asked.

Anna looked at the vast building in front of her.

'Where would he have put all those millions of bricks if God had given all the money at once?'

George Müller looked down from an upstairs window on the crocodile of children walking two by two up the drive to Ashley Down.

'How many will live here?' asked the stranger who stood beside him.

'Three hundred,' Müller replied, 'compared to the hundred and fifty we were able to care for in Wilson Street.'

'Who funds the operation?' the man queried.

Müller turned from watching the children and looked at the man.

'The Lord funds the operation. Every penny we need comes from him.'

'Yes, I know that,' the man said impatiently. 'But how do you make your needs known so that your God will provide for them?'

George Müller shook his head. 'We don't advertise our needs. We don't need to. God knows them all.'

'Look here,' the stranger said, 'I came here as a neighbour of Ashley Down intending to give a generous donation to the running of the Home, but you are almost obstructive in your avoidance of answering my questions.'

'My good sir,' Müller said, again looking out the window as the last of the line of children reached the top of the drive, 'Let me explain. We have never asked anyone for money nor have we held any fund-raising activities. Our needs are made known only to the Lord, and he opens the hearts of generous people who respond by giving gifts to cover all our needs. Since the first home opened not one child has gone hungry, been cold for lack of blankets or adequate clothing.'

'And all that has been done without appealing for funds?'

'All that,' agreed Müller, 'and much, much more.'

The stranger rose to his feet and walked from side to side of the room.

'Poor man,' thought Müller, 'he doesn't know how to cope with this. He only knows about funding from a human point of view.'

'I came here to ask you what you needed and you would not tell me,' the man said to Müller. 'It was my intention to give you up to £200 for the work you are doing but I cannot give to needs I don't understand. In any case it seems that you have your God at your beck and call. You don't need a mere £200 from me. I have no doubt he will provide for all your needs. How I wish I had your faith. Good day, sir.'

'Have you asked him for it?' George Müller asked.

The man stopped with his hand on the door handle. 'Asked who for what?'

'Have you asked God for the gift of faith?'

'Is your God able to answer all requests?'

'I don't believe that he has ever refused to give anyone who asked for it the gift of faith.'

'You have given me much to think about, Mr Müller. Good day, sir.'

'Seek and you will find,' George said, but the door was closed.

The following day George had another visitor.

'Will you show Mr James around the Orphan House,' Müller asked Walter Cotton, a fourteen year old who had been in his care for several years. 'He has come a long way just to see it.'

Walter was glad to oblige.

'Are you happy?' the visitor asked.

Walter looked at him. 'Yes sir,' he said, a little surprised at the question.

Mr James pursued the subject. 'Are all the children happy?'

'Why, yes,' the boy said. Then he thought about his answer. 'Well, maybe not all,' he admitted. 'Some don't like it here.'

'Why is that?'

'The ones who don't settle usually have lost their parents when they were older and they remember being happy at home with them. But most of us don't remember having homes of our own, and some, like me, do but don't want to.'

'May I ask what you mean?'

The boy shrugged. 'I don't remember my mother. She died of cholera. My father was all right when sober but that wasn't often. When he was drunk he beat me.'

Mr James's face softened.

'He was killed when he ran in front of a horse and Mr Müller took me in. I'm happier here than I ever was at home.'

Walter opened his dormitory door to let the visitor in.

'My dear sir,' Mr James said, when Walter had shown him back into the Director's office over an hour later. 'I came here to criticise and I've come now to praise.'

George asked him to sit down and explain himself.

'It seemed to me that no institution as large as yours could provide a homely atmosphere for children to grow up in. But I've been shown that's not the case by young Walter and his friends.'

'I'm glad about that,' said Müller.

'And I expected to see boys' and girls' needs met at a very basic level. Instead I discovered children happy and content, well-dressed and with their hair cut attractively. They are a credit to you, sir. You are like a father to them.'

George Müller looked his visitor in the eye.

'They are not,' he said a little stiffly. 'They are a credit to their Heavenly Father who has provided for all their needs to be met, including their need to be happy and their need to have dignity and self-respect.'

'If what you say is true,' Mr James concluded, 'then my perception of God has been rather limited. Goodbye.'

'I think it has,' Müller thought, as his visitor left, 'but he may surprise you yet. I pray that he will.'

'What do you like best about Ashley Down?' Anna asked Isabella some months later.

'I think I like the space and the light. What about you?'

'My favourite thing is that all the children can have their outside playtime together. In Wilson Street, when only one house could go out at a time, I never saw my cousins. Now we can play together and talk about our families.'

Isabella laughed. 'And I like to see the white things lying in the sun on the bleaching green, and the clothes blowing in the wind. Sometimes the rows of nightshirts look as if they are dancing together.'

'And another thing I like is the garden,' added Anna, 'especially the flowers.'

'Trees are better than flowers,' Isabella laughed. 'You can't climb up a bluebell.'

'What would Miss Fletcher say if she caught you up a tree?'

Anna looked at her friend. 'You've changed a lot.'

'What do you mean?' Isabella asked.

'When you arrived in Wilson Street everything frightened you. Now you don't even mind Miss Fletcher catching you up a tree.'

'I'd had a lot to be frightened of.'

'What kind of things?' the inquisitive Anna asked.

Isabella sighed. 'Things happened to me when I was little that I don't want to talk about.' She shivered despite the warmth of the autumn sun. 'And when I was taken into the Orphan Home I was frightened that I'd be sent away if I did anything wrong.'

'Mr Müller doesn't send orphans away!' Anna said in a horrified voice.

'I know that now ... but it was different then. I remember a day or two after arriving at the Home waking up in the morning thinking I was in heaven because nobody was drinking gin or fighting or shouting or hurting.'

Anna listened, wide-eyed.

'And I thought if I was bad I'd not be able to stay in heaven and someone would throw me out. That's why I was always so worried.'

'You're not at all like that now.'

'No,' Isabella agreed, 'Thanks to Mr Müller. After I'd been in the Home for about a year I met him one day in the corridor and he asked me if I was happy. When I told him that the Home was like heaven he sat down and talked to me about the real heaven. Mr Müller prayed with me and I gave my heart to Jesus. So now I have a safe home here on earth and a home for ever in heaven too. That's why I'm not frightened now.'

'I can see that,' said Anna. 'But why did people hurt you when you were little.'

Shaking her head, Isabella grabbed the lowest branch of a tree and swung on in. 'I don't want to talk about it . It doesn't matter any more.'

Anna looked all around and, as there was no sign of Miss Fletcher, she did a run and jump, caught the same branch as her friend, and they swung on it together.

―――――――――

'How bright these glorious spirits shine!
Whence all their white array?
How came they to the blissful seats
Of everlasting day?
Lo! these are they, from sufferings great
Who came to realms of light,
And in the blood of Christ have washed
Those robes which shine so bright.'
Isaac Watts

―――――――――

Home-goings

'A second Orphan House! However many orphans do you think need our care?' asked Robert Baker, who worked at Ashley Down.

'There are vast multitudes. Someone told me some years ago that there were at that time six thousand young orphans in prison in England because there was nowhere else to keep them,' Müller said.

'But we cannot take on sole care of all the orphans in the country.'

'No,' agreed Müller, 'but I have a vision of a thousand of them here at Ashley Down. There is space. And if it is the Lord's will he will provide both the bricks and mortar for the buildings and the bread and milk for the children.'

Six years later George Müller and Robert Baker walked the corridors of House No 2, examining the new-fangled fittings.

'I confess I don't understand how this gas lighting works,' Baker said, 'but it is very effective.'

'And the central heating,' asked Müller, 'do you think it is adequate to keep the children warm in the winter?'

Thinking of the size of the boiler, Baker replied. 'They'll be the cosiest children in Bristol.'

In November 1857 the new Orphan House was opened, providing a home for four hundred children.

The work went on from strength to strength. George recorded, 'In September 1858 I obtained 11½ acres of land close to New Orphan Houses No 1 and No 2, and only separated from them by the road. On these 11½ acres a house was built. ... After having had several meetings with the architects, and finding that it was possible to accommodate with comparatively little more expense 450 orphans, instead of 400, I finally decided on that number, so as to have eventually 1,150 orphans under my care, instead of 1000.'

'Are you in a great deal of pain?' George asked his wife as she struggled to get out of her chair.

It was 1859, and throughout the twenty-nine years of their marriage she had supported her husband in all he did.

'It is difficult today,' she admitted, 'I think it's the damp weather that makes it so bad.'

She looked at her swollen and inflamed knuckles. 'But it will pass.'

'I think you should stay in the warmth of your bed for a day or two,' suggested George.'

Mary smiled weakly. 'Perhaps you are right.'

He helped her to their room, neither of them guessing that it would be nine months before she would be fit to move about again.'

'I feel so helpless,' Mary said to her husband

one morning. 'You are busier than ever and I seem to be able to do nothing at all.'

George sat on the edge of her bed and took her disfigured hand in his.

'What is the basis of the work we do?' he asked.

'Why, prayer,' she answered, 'and God's willingness to hear and answer.'

'And do you need hands that can embroider to pray?' he went on.

Mary smiled and shook her head. 'No,' she said, resolutely, 'I don't. You're quite right. Even from my bed I can be fully involved in the work. Just tell me each day what should be taken to the Lord in prayer, and I'll take it to him.'

And that was what happened.

George stood at his study window in Ashley Down one afternoon the following year when the children were at play. Mary sat in a chair by the fire. It was the first time she had managed to sit there since her bad attack of rheumatism. There was laughter and singing, chasing and tag. Many games of football were underway. Some of the older girls organised games for the smallest orphans. Boys marched like soldiers and romped like puppies. Müller's eyes roamed over the scene, settling first on one group and then another.

'There's Anna,' he said. 'How she's grown. And Isabella is beside her as usual. It rejoices my soul each time I see her. From a fearful child who thought an Orphan Home was heaven, Anna has grown into a fine girl whose heart is in heaven, and whose faith shines through everything she does. There she is now, with a little one in her arms.'

That's what makes all this worthwhile,' said Mary.

'And there's William weeding among the shrubs. Another few months and he'll be apprenticed. We must try to find a gardener who'll take him on. He's happiest when his hands are in the earth and the sun's on his back.

'Little wonder' George said, remembering the desperate state he'd been in when he arrived at the Orphan Home, covered in lice and plagued by worms.

'It still surprises me,' Mary commented, 'how often we've been able to find just the right job for the older orphans when they have left our care. I'm quite sure a gardener will be looking for an apprentice when William's time comes.'

'Ashley Down's a great help in that respect,' said George. 'The older children get such wide experiences in the laundry, the kitchen, the bakery, the garden, looking after the hens ... and helping look after the little children too, of course.'

His wife laughed. 'You make it sound like slave labour.'

Müller looked out of the window.

'Does that look and sound like a slave?' he asked.

Below them William continued weeding the flower bed. He was whistling happily as he worked. Suddenly aware of being watched, the boy stopped what he was doing, turned towards their window and waved.

There was a knock at the door.

'Come in,' Müller called, laying down his pen.

A couple came in with their son.

'Do you remember me, sir?' asked the young man.

'How could I forget,' George smiled as he shook their hands. 'Our orphans are part of our family your know, even when they grow up and leave us.'

'John Woodman and Agnes, how good to see you both,' Mary said warmly. 'And is this fine young lad your son?'

'Yes, sir,' John said proudly. 'He's called Harry.'

'How old are you, Harry?' asked Mary Müller.

'I am ten and three quarters,' the boy answered smartly.

John took a package from his inside coat pocket. 'We would like you to use this for the orphans,' he said, handing it to Müller. 'We hear you hope to care for two thousand of them eventually.'

'God willing, that's what we hope to do,' George agreed, opening the envelope. Inside there were five one-pound notes.

'There must be a story behind such a generous gift as this' he said, looking up at the couple.

It was John who explained. 'You did well when you apprenticed me to the farrier at Brookfield House. I loved working with the horses and the farrier did a good job of training me. Then when

Agnes came to work in the big house as a scullery maid, I discovered what real happiness was.'

His wife smiled at the memory.

'We saw each other on our day off each week, and sometimes when the farrier gave me messages to take to the kitchen. His wife was the under-cook. And to cut a long story short, Mr Müller, we married and tried to make as happy a home as you gave us in your children's homes.'

Realising that George Müller was struggling with tears, his wife asked the Woodmans what happened next.

'When the farrier retired John was promoted to his position and we now have our own little cottage near the stables.'

Müller had himself under control.

'And do you like the horses, Harry?'

'I do, sir,' he said. 'When I'm a man I want to be a coachman, with my own grey mares.'

John coughed. 'And since I was promoted we have put a little aside each week as the Lord made us able for the care of poor orphan children such as we once were.'

'It's not much,' Agnes said, 'among so many.'

'But it is worth more than you'll ever know,' Müller told them.

'Come now, Harry,' John said. 'Mr Müller is a busy man.'

John ushered his son out of the door.

'He has your eyes, Agnes,' Mary Müller said. 'Brown and deep and kind.'

Long after the door had closed behind the

Woodmans, Müller sat at his desk.

'Some of the most precious gifts we've been given are for the smallest sums of money,' he said.

Reaching down a folder, he took out a letter. 'Remember this?' he asked.

'Dear Sir, Will you be pleased to accept this small gift as from the Lord. ... I have had it in my heart to help you, but had not the means. Last year, however, I said to my husband, we will give to the Lord one of our young hens; and I now enclose you 1s 8d in postage stamps, the sale of her first eggs. We send it for the Mission Fund. I wish to tell you that my husband is a poor working man, with five children.'

Mary nodded.

'Thank you, Father,' Müller prayed, 'for every penny you have given for the orphans and the missionary work, for the schools and Sunday schools, and for the distribution of Scriptures. It is you, Lord, who has moved the hearts of all who have given, whether thousands of pounds or a young hen. Thank you especially today for John and Agnes and Harry. They are tokens of your blessing on the orphan work. And thank you most of all for the Lord Jesus Christ, who died to save the souls of poor sinners, and to adopt them into your great family on earth and in heaven. Amen.'

'Amen,' echoed his wife.

'It has done me good to come today, George,' said Mary, 'but I think it is time I went home now.'

Just over five years later, on 22nd January 1866, George wrote in his diary.

'This evening, about half-past eleven, my beloved fellow-labourer and intimate friend for thirty-six years, Henry Craik, fell asleep, after an illness of seven months.'

'We may not be long after him,' said Mary, when she heard of Henry's death.

There was a great sadness in their home that night, relieved only by the knowledge that they would one day meet again in heaven.

'Let's sing,' suggested Mary.

Their voices blended in Isaac Watts' hymn.

'How bright these glorious spirits shine!
Whence all their white array?
How came they to the blissful seats
Of everlasting day?
Lo! these are they, from sufferings great
Who came to realms of light,
And in the blood of Christ have washed
Those robes which shine so bright.'

The work on the fourth house went on and the building was completed and opened on 5th November, 1868.

'Listen to this,' George said to Mary, on arriving home early one evening the following year. 'It's from some of the grown up orphan boys who've remained at Ashley Down to help the school-teachers in House No 4.

'Dear and honoured Sir,' he read, 'Please accept

our warmest thanks for your kindness in placing us in the position of pupil teachers. We hope, by the help of God, to be able to maintain our position, and also by working hard to rise in our calling. We thank you very much for allowing us sixpence weekly. We all like our present occupation, and hope, as time proceeds, to like it more and more; and we hope to grow in the grace and knowledge of God our Father and of the Lord Jesus Christ. We have found the word of the Psalmist fulfilled to the letter, when he said, *When my father and my mother forsake me, then the Lord will take me up*. The Lord has indeed taken us up, and placed us under your fatherly care and protection, and has also given us advantages above the ordinary run of orphan boys. But in one sense we are not orphans; for we have a Father in heaven, whose tender care and protection will shield us from all the fiery darts of the wicked one. Please accept our kindest wishes, that God would yet spare your life many years, to carry out his own work. We remain, dear Sir, yours respectfully, *The Pupil Teachers of No 4*.'

Mary's face was bathed in joy.

'How good God is,' she said. 'He has answered our prayers.'

On 6th January, 1870, Mary Müller was in a state of great weakness.

'The long-longed-for, and the long-prayed-for day has arrived,' her husband said. 'Today's the day New Orphan House No 5 is opened.'

Despite having lain awake most of the night she smiled at his early morning enthusiasm.

'All the expenses in connection with No 4 and No 5 being built, fitted up, and furnished, have been met to the full,' he went on, sitting on her bed. 'And, now that everything is paid, we are left with a balance of several thousand pounds.'

'Praise the Lord!' said Mary.

George looked at his wife.

'I wonder how much longer we are going to praise God together on earth?' He wondered, seeing her grey complexion and her deep-sunk eyes.

Exactly a month later, at 4 o'clock in the afternoon of 6th February, 1870, Mary Müller died. They had been married for over 39 years, and had served the Lord together faithfully.

Of the funeral, George wrote, 'Today the earthly remains of my precious wife were laid in the grave. Many thousands of people showed their deepest sympathy. About 1200 of the orphans, who were able to walk, followed in the procession; the whole staff of helpers at the Orphan Houses who could be spared, and hundreds of believers of the church with which she had been in communion. I, myself, with God's help, performed the service.'

George Müller

'I often think of that, and am amazed at God's choice of such a weak and helpless person as myself. And when I cast my mind back over the years to my youth in Prussia, I'm speechless with wonder at his taking a lying, drinking, cheating thief and entrusting him with over a million pounds.'

George Müller

Wedding Bells

George's mind wandered from his papers. He looked out of his office window into the August sunshine.

'How Mary would have loved to see the flowers,' he thought. 'What a difference a year and a half makes to a garden.'

There was a knock at the door.

'May I speak to you please?'

It was James Wright, George's assistant.

'Certainly,' the older man replied, pushing his chair pack from his desk. 'Sit down and tell me what's on your mind.'

Wright coughed nervously.

'It is a matter of some delicacy,' he began.

George waited.

'Mr Müller, I have come to. ask for your daughter's hand in marriage.'

'Marriage? I had no idea! How blind can a father be!'

'Have you asked Lydia?'

'I have.'

'And her answer?'

'She took two weeks to say yes.'

'Did she give you a reason for her delay in accepting?'

Wright hesitated. 'Yes,' he admitted. 'She is concerned about leaving you alone so soon after Mrs Müller's death.'

'Dear girl, how kind of her ... but how mistaken,' George said. 'I've appreciated her company and her help so much but I'll not stand between her and a happy marriage. How sad it would be if my precious wife's home-call to heaven would prevent my daughter becoming a wife at all.'

James Wright looked very relieved.

'Are you happy?' George asked Lydia after dinner that evening.

The sun bathed them in its warmth.

'Yes,' she smiled. 'I am. I couldn't find a better husband than James. We know each other so well that we are comfortable together as well as being in love. But ... '

'Yes?'

'But I'm worried about you,' Lydia confessed.

'Why?' Müller asked.

'It means you'll be left alone for the first time since you and Mother were married.'

'Listen, my dear,' George said. 'Do you think that I'd deprive you of the happiness of married life just to add to the comfort of my old age?'

His daughter said nothing.

'And do you think that the God who promises to care for the widow won't care for the widower?'

Lydia smiled. 'How typical of him to say that,' she thought.

'Or perhaps you think I'm just helpless!'

'There are over a thousand children out there who would happily help you if you were!' she laughed. 'And every one of them loves you.'

Müller nodded. 'I may be alone after you are married,' he said. 'But I have no excuse for being lonely.'

'And you have three months and twelve days to prove to me you're not helpless!' teased Lydia.

Her father closed his eyes against the setting sun.

'I'll do my best,' he assured her.

Some weeks later George, Lydia and James Wright arranged to have lunch together in Müller's office.

'Please make sure we are not disturbed,' George told Lily, who served their meal.

She closed the door firmly behind her.

A look of concern passed between the young couple.

'James,' said his future father-in-law, 'I am sure you count it a great blessing to be marrying again after the death of your first wife.'

'I do indeed, sir. It is a gift I never thought to have. When she died part of my heart died with her. I know you'll understand that.'

Müller sighed. 'Yes,' he agreed, 'I do. And I hope that both of you will understand my situation and what I have decided to do.'

Lydia's brow furrowed.

Her father went on. 'In the light of your marriage, and for a whole variety of other reasons, I too have decided to marry again.'

There was silence in the room until Lydia spoke.

'Who are you going to marry, Father?'

'I don't think you'll be surprised when I tell you that my future wife is Miss Susannah Grace Sangar.'

He watched his daughter's expression change from one of concern to one of real pleasure.

'I can't remember a time when she wasn't a friend,' Lydia said. 'She's almost part of the family already.'

Wright rose to his feet, grasped Müller's hand and shook it warmly. 'I'm pleased for you, sir, really pleased.'

George's face, which had worn a tense expression all morning, relaxed into a smile.

'When will you be married?' Lydia asked.

'Well, my dear,' he replied, 'as you think I'm such a hopeless case we have decided to be married just two weeks after you, on 30th November. Do you think I'll survive the fortnight?'

'With a little help,' Lydia laughed. 'But I shouldn't risk leaving it any longer than that. You may need clean clothes!'

So, in November 1871, two weddings took place and two marriages began.

'It seems the right time to make James my Co-Director,' George told Susannah in the spring of the following year.

124

'Tell me your thinking,' she encouraged.

Müller sat down. 'It's hard to know where to begin,' he said. 'It's not because he's my son-in-law, that's a fact. I've known James from boyhood. And for the last twenty years I've had the privilege of watching his growth in Christian grace. His life is a reflection of his Master's. Over the twelve years he has worked alongside me I've been impressed by his concern for the children and his practical good sense. So much so that just after he came here to work Mary and I noted him as a possible successor and we prayed for him until the very day she died.'

Susannah nodded. 'Mary often talked in these terms. And it may interest you to know that you were not the only ones praying for him.'

'I know that.'

'But go on with your narrative,' she said. 'I always find that it helps clarify things if I go through them from beginning to end. You may find the same.'

'After Mary died I approached James regarding the matter. His response was typical of his humility. He found all sorts of reasons why he wasn't fit for the job. And his wife, who was then still in the best of health, felt it too great a burden for him. But God changed her mind and eventually he came to me saying that he could no longer refuse. Soon afterwards, as you know, his dear wife died. So the matter was determined before there was any question of him marrying Lydia.'

'So what are you saying?'

Müller nodded. 'You were quite right. Seeing the whole picture makes the matter clear. The time has come to appoint James as Co-Director and my successor. What a relief that is!'

George Müller and James Wright settled down to work together. The arrangement was a good one. It allowed the older man to shed some of the responsibility and eased the younger man towards his succession.

George was in his room at Ashley Down at the end of March 1874 when he heard someone running along the corridor.

'Father, come quickly,' said Lydia, bursting into his room at Ashley Down. 'Susannah's very ill.'

'What's happened?' he asked as he rose from his desk and grabbed his coat.

'She's had a haemorrhage,' his daughter explained. 'Doctor Williams is on his way.'

They rushed home, arriving just before the doctor. Having spent some time with his patient he spoke to George seriously.

'Mrs Müller is gravely ill.'

'Is her life at risk?'

'She may not recover. The next days are critical.'

George was silent.

'I'll do everything I can but you must pray, man. God can help where I can't.'

George sat with his wife, praying as she tossed restlessly in bed. 'Grant her sleep, Lord,' he prayed. 'You promised to give your beloved sleep.'

And eventually, in a state of complete exhaustion, Susannah lapsed into quietness and sleep.

'She's not out of the woods yet,' the doctor said the following morning. 'All I can say is that she has a better chance of survival today than she had yesterday. But I don't think I've ever known anyone recover from such a serious haemorrhage.'

'With God all things are possible,' George quoted.

The doctor risked a smile. 'Even the very improbable.'

Susannah did survive. Two months after collapsing, she was well enough to go with her husband to Somerset to recuperate there. And on their return she set to work helping in the Orphan Homes.

Ten years later, in 1884, Müller and Wright sat at opposite sides of George's study desk.

'I never thought I would see this day,' George said, and it gives me the greatest of pleasure that you are here to share it with me.'

'Let's check the arithmetic again,' James suggested, 'although I know it is correct.'

Müller took up his pen.

'By 1st January this year we had been given for the Lord's work the sum of one million, eight thousand three hundred and eighty pounds. Now tell me the gifts since then.'

'£10 for the school fund from Paddington,' James said, '£50 for missions, £50 for the orphans, £10 for your own expenses.'

George wrote down the figures.

'£100 from Hampshire for the Bible and Mission Fund, £200 for the orphans and another £50 for your needs. Then there was £50 from Sussex for Missions and a further £100 for the orphans. After that came the gift of £1000, £500 of which was for the orphans. What does that come to?' he asked.

'In the fifty years since the work was begun the total we have been given in gifts is one million and ten thousand pounds.'

'I was sure of it!' said the delighted James. 'How good God is. How faithful he is to all his promises.'

George looked at his son-in-law. 'You and I have special cause to thank him for keeping his promises.'

'Indeed we have,' James agreed. 'Our Heavenly Father, who promises to look after the widow and the fatherless has given us both happy marriages out of our widowhood, and has used us to care for some many fatherless and motherless children.'

'I often think of that, and am amazed at God's choice of a weak and helpless person like me. When I cast my mind back over the years to my youth in Prussia, I'm speechless with wonder at his taking a lying, drinking, cheating thief and entrusting him with over a million pounds.'

'You've come a long way since then.'

'God has held my hand every step of the way.'

♦ ♦ ♦

'How lovely to see you, Lydia,' her father said, as she came into the room one day the following spring. 'Let's have tea together, Susannah.'

His wife left the two together in front of the fire, returning a little while later with tea and hot crumpets.

Müller smiled. 'I'm being well looked after as you can see.'

'I'm glad to hear it!' Lydia laughed, taking a bite of crumpet before the butter melted and ran off it. 'What a treat. And I have another treat for you after tea.'

'What's that?' her father asked.

'You'll have to wait until you've washed your buttery hands,' Lydia said.

George did as he was told.

'Come then,' he said, on returning to the room, 'what have you got to show me?'

Lydia took an envelope from her bag. 'This came this morning. James asked me to bring it to you. He recognised the handwriting and said it would do your soul good.'

George opened the letter and read aloud.

'Beloved Sir, Once more it is the privilege of one of your former orphans to ask your acceptance of this small offering of thanksgiving to God for all his loving kindness to me and mine. I need hardly say, that, as each year passes away, my respect for you, dear Sir, and love for the dear place where I spent the best part of my childhood, increases, so also I hope does my gratitude to the Father of the fatherless, who put it in the heart of you, his honoured and beloved servant, to carry out such a noble scheme to the glory of God. How often, when tempted to indulge in the sin of unbelief, has the thought of my six years' stay at Ashley Down come across my mind like a gleam of sunshine. There, the clothes I wore, the food I ate, the bed I slept on, and the walls around me, were all in answer to believing prayer. What better prescription for any unbeliever, than to go to Ashley Down Orphan House and enquire into its working! And what better prescription for the doubting, wavering child of God!'

A gift of ten shillings was enclosed.

'Thanks be to God,' Müller said. 'He provided every penny.'

George Müller

'I remember the day she was born and that very day I prayed for the salvation of her soul, a prayer that was repeated every day until she was born again as a thirteen year old. My heart rejoiced even more at her rebirth than at her birth.'
George Müller speaking about his daughter Lydia.

200,000 miles
in seventeen years!

'What a man your Father is!' Susannah told Lydia. 'He seems to have boundless energy.'

Her step-daughter nodded.

'Tell me about the preaching tour.'

'We left, as you know on 27th March 1875, exactly one hundred days ago. We've visited Brighton, Sunderland, Newcastle-upon-Tyne and London. Your father preached seventy times, and his congregations were sometimes as large as three thousand people. For a man of seventy he does extraordinarily well.'

'He certainly seems to have taken to a travelling ministry,' Lydia agreed. 'How soon is it until you leave on his next preaching tour?'

Susannah took a deep breath. 'Just five weeks,' she said. 'And such a lot has to be done before then because we are to be away for eleven months.'

Lydia looked a little surprised.

'What do I pack for that length of time?' asked Susannah.

Lydia laughed. 'Everything, I imagine!'

'I was afraid you would say that,' Susannah

said, laughing along with her step-daughter.

'You'll write to me and keep me in touch with what is going on here,' George instructed James Wright during their last meeting before he and Susannah left.

'Yes,' James agreed. 'I'll do that.'

'I can't tell you what it means to be able to leave you in charge here,' Müller told his son-in-law. 'I can go away with an easy mind.'

'I have to admit it is a daunting thought that you'll be away for nearly a year.'

'Our trust is in God not in men,' George said. 'And he remains faithful whether I am here or there.'

'Where exactly is 'there' going to be?'

Müller smiled. 'This tour takes us throughout England, Scotland and Ireland,' he explained. 'And if God wills and my health permits I have invitations to tour Europe for a year from next summer and Canada and the United States thereafter, from August 1877 to July 1878.'

'It seems that I'm going to have to get used to your being 'there' rather than here!' James concluded.

Müller agreed.

And that is how it was for the following fifteen years. James and Lydia worked in Bristol while George and Susannah toured the world. Despite his age Müller preached with all his heart.

'Even Father's travels benefit the orphans,' Lydia told James as they worked in the office together. 'Here is $100 from America with a most interesting letter to Father.'

James raised his eyes from the accounts and sat back in his chair.

'I send you herewith a cheque for $100, to be used for yourself or for any work you have in hand,' she read. 'I shall always thank the Lord for my having met with you; and I pray that many days may be added to your life. Will you do me the kindness to offer one earnest prayer for myself, my wife, and our three children, that we all may be saved? Pray also, that the Lord will bless me in my business, as he has condescended to give me grace to use what he gives me for his glory. It may be interesting to you to know my plan of giving, which I think the best, and unlike any of which I know. Our State (Virginia) was the great battlefield, and, having lost the slaves, and having left a poor farm only, I being young, studied law. I resolved to give 5% of my net income (after paying all expenses) until worth $5,000; then 10% till worth $10,000; then 15% until worth $15,000; and so on, increasing 5% on each $5,000 till I should be worth $50,000, and then, after that, all that I make in the way of profits. If the Lord will continue to bless me, I shall in a very few years come to this limit, and will then, God helping me, give all my profits to his work. I think that a Christian should not lay up more than is necessary, but that, the Lord having given him what is necessary, I should ask no more, and give all else to the work of the Lord. I have written this not in any wise to call attention to myself, but, because I consider it the true principle of benevolence, and one that will be attended with blessing.'

'Your father will be interested in his thinking,' James said.

'I'll put this letter with all the others that are waiting for him. What a pile there is!'

'And we owe it to our American friend to pray for him and his family.'

The couple knelt at the leather couch on which Müller had often poured out his heart in prayer. And they were in no hurry to rise.

♦ ♦ ♦

'Are you all right?' James asked his wife one day in the autumn of 1889.

She was sitting beside the fire with her eyes closed.

'Yes,' she said a little wearily, 'I was just snatching a few minutes to pray for Father. They'll be in India by now. I was thinking just the other day about the travelling they have done. In the fourteen years since his seventieth birthday they have been in Europe three times, including a tour in Russia, Canada and the United States four times, the Middle East, India twice, Australia twice, China, Japan, New Zealand and Ceylon. They have been away for a total of nearly nine years and much of the time they have been in England has been spent on his preaching tours here.' Lydia smiled. 'It tires me even to think of it.'

'You do look tired,' James said, with a note of concern in his voice.

'It'll pass. But I wish I had a fraction of Father's energy.'

But it did not pass. Lydia's lethargy was the early sign of an illness.

She was still in bed one morning when James brought her a letter from Müller.

'Would you read it to me?' she asked.

He sat on the edge of the bed and opened the flimsy envelope carefully.

'It's from India,' he said.

Lydia nodded. But she did not open her eyes.

'My dear daughter and son-in-law,' he read, 'After the monsoons had set in, and this excessive heat been a little decreased, so that travelling would not be so dangerous (humanly speaking), we left Darjeeling to go to Simla, a beautiful town of the Himalayan mountains, in order that I might preach at Simla also to the thousands of inhabitants and visitors there assembled. This long railway journey from Darjeeling to Simla, via Calcutta, of about sixteen hundred miles, was connected with many trials, but the Lord carried us through them. We stayed ten weeks and four days at Simla, and then left for Mussourie, another town on the Himalayan mountains, where we stayed from September 21st until October 14th. Whilst at Darjeeling, at Simla, and at Mussourie, I had not only an abundance of opportunities of preaching to Europeans, to Eurasians, and to Americans; but also to educated natives in

English, and to the uneducated natives too with translation into the Hindustani language. I sought likewise to make good use of the opportunities thus afforded to me of meeting the very great number of missionary brethren and sisters coming from the plains to the mountains, and to strengthen their hands in God.'

He turned the page. 'How does he do it?' he asked. There was no reply. Lydia was fast asleep.

Wright looked at his wife. Her face was grey against the white pillows and even in sleep she looked pained. The thought of what was happening to her tore at his heart.

♦ ♦ ♦

'Don't you think we should tell your father how unwell you are?' James asked some weeks later.

Lydia considered the question. 'No,' she said. 'Whatever happens Father knows I am safe in the arms of Jesus. Whether our Heavenly Father takes me home sooner or later is not what matters. What matters is that when he calls, I'll go to him, and will be with him forever.'

James nodded. He could not trust himself to speak.

'I know in my heart that I'm not long for this world,' she said tenderly. 'My only sadness is that my family will miss me. I can't feel anything but a quiet calmness about my home-going.'

Her husband found his voice. 'That's the Lord's gift of his peace, the peace that passes all understanding.'

Lydia nodded her agreement. 'And it will keep you too in the difficult days ahead.'

While James knew that was true, he felt a deep sadness in his heart at the thought of losing his wife.

On 10th January 1890, Lydia Wright, was called home to heaven. She was 57 years old.

George Müller was preaching in India when a missionary asked to speak to him.

'I have sad news for you,' he explained, handing him a letter.

Müller sat down, opened the envelope, and read of the death of his daughter. James had let the missionary know by telegram.

'The Lord gave and the Lord has taken away,' George said in a quiet but firm voice. 'Blessed be the name of the Lord.'

He returned home to his lodgings.

'Of course we must go home,' Susannah agreed, when she heard the news and they had spent some time in prayer together. 'But others can make the arrangements. We need time to be quiet and time to talk.'

'Yes,' George sighed, 'your way of talking through things from beginning to end does help things to stay in perspective.'

'I'm grateful,' said Susannah, 'that although we didn't marry until Lydia was grown-up that I knew her from quite a young age.'

'I remember the day she was born,' Müller said. 'And that very day I prayed for the salvation of her soul, a prayer that was repeated every day until she was born again as a thirteen year old. My heart rejoiced even more at her rebirth than at her birth. Which is why I can rejoice through my sadness at her death.'

'She was a good daughter,' Susannah added, 'and a splendid wife to James.'

'He will miss her sorely. Their lives' work bound them together almost as much as their marriage. They have laboured together with the orphans for over thirty years.'

Two weeks after Lydia's death her father and step mother left Jubbulpore for Bombay from where, after preaching sixteen times in three weeks, they boarded a ship bound for Europe.

'When we returned to Bristol,' George recorded in his diary, 'I had great cause for praise, that the whole work was going on so well under the direction of Mr Wright.'

'I am most grateful for your help over these last four months since you came home from India,' James told his father-in-law. 'I don't think I could have coped without you.'

'It has done me good to be back among the children and to see for myself how the Lord continues to provide for them without anyone asking for as much as a penny. But I'm needing a rest now. Four months has been long enough. Remember I'm an old man.

Wright looked at Müller. 'You are the youngest eighty-four-year-old I know.'

'That's as may be but we've been here long enough. Susannah and I are leaving for Germany soon. We'll have a holiday then I'll preach there and in Switzerland until next summer.'

'Are you fit to continue your preaching tours?'

'Yes,' George said, 'I believe God still has work for me to do. And I can think of no better way of using my last years than in his service.

'Lydia was just like you in that respect,' James commented. 'She worked for the orphans for as long as her strength lasted. Then, when she was no longer able to do practical things she continued to give the benefit of her long years of experience. And right to the end she prayed. How she prayed. I would wake in the night and hear her whispering to the Lord about this child or that, or calling down his blessing on your ministry.'

'It was a privilege to be her father.'

'She was especially prayerful towards the end,' Wright went on, 'that those of us she left should not grieve her passing too deeply, but rather rest assured that she was in glory with her lovely and loving Lord Jesus.'

Müller considered this before answering. 'Her prayers were answered in India. When we received the letter telling us of her death both Susannah and I, though deeply saddened, felt an overwhelming peace.'

'And her prayers were answered in Bristol too,' the younger man said.

'We have a prayer-hearing and a prayer-answering God,' George announced, standing up to go, 'and that fact has been the basis of the work for the past sixty years.'

'Situations change, you see, and God provides for the needs of today not for the needs as they were yesterday or twenty years ago.'
George Müller on God's continued provision.

Face to face with Jesus

'Mr Müller!' children's voices called from behind.

George stopped walking and turned round. Five boys were running in his direction.

'Who'll win the race?' he asked.

Walter made a huge effort. 'I won!' he panted, sinking at the man's feet.

'I think that my old legs need a rest as much as your young ones do although it's many years since I ran a race. Let's sit under this tree till you get your breath back, then you can tell me what you want.'

'How long are you home for this time, sir?' Fred was first to recover.

'Mrs Müller and I leave again in two months.'

'Please sir, where are you going then?' enquired Walter.

'We are off to Germany,' George told them. 'That's where I was born.'

♦ ♦ ♦

'Isn't that a lovely picture?' Miss Fletcher asked her colleague. Miss Archer looked towards the oak tree in the corner of the garden and nodded.

'He has such patience with the children,' she said. 'You would never think he was nearly ninety. He sits with his back as straight as a young man and I'm sure the suit he wore when he married dear Mrs Mary Müller would still fit him. He's not gained any weight at all over the years.'

'Unlike me,' complained Miss Archer, thinking of her steadily increasing waistline. 'But it's his eyes that make him stand out. I've never known a man with more kindly eyes than his.'

'I think that's why all the children love him. When he speaks to them he looks right at them and they can't take their eyes off his.'

Miss Archer thought for a moment. 'I suppose you could say that his eyes had been the means of a child being converted.'

'When was that?'

'Don't you remember the boy who was to be expelled?'

'That narrows it down to just a few over the years,' said Miss Fletcher, casting her mind back.

Miss Archer went on. 'Mr Müller put his hand on the boy's head and prayed for him. Instead of closing his eyes the impudent lad stared defiantly at Mr Müller and saw that the dear man had tears running down his face.'

'I remember,' her friend said. 'The boy was converted in the act of being expelled. And needless to say he wasn't sent away after all.'

'I wonder what they're talking about,' said Miss Archer, looking across the grass to the little group under the oak tree. 'I wonder.'

♦ ♦ ♦

'Please sir,' Fred asked, 'will you tell us how you first came to look after orphans?'

'The orphan homes are part of a much bigger picture,' George Müller explained to the boys on the grass around him. 'When Mr Craik and I founded The Scripture Knowledge Institution our aims were to help Sunday Schools, and to found day schools and schools for adults where the students would learn about the Lord during the week as well as on Sundays.'

'Just like we do here at Ashley Down,' said Walter.

Müller nodded his agreement. 'We also aimed to distribute the Scriptures as widely as possible and our final aim was to help missionaries in whatever way we could.'

Fred looked puzzled. 'But what about us? You didn't even mention orphans.'

'That came a little later,' the old man explained, 'when the cholera hit Bristol and so many children were left orphans as a result of it.'

'So building a home for orphans became another of your aims,' concluded Walter.

Müller chose his words carefully. 'Not exactly,' he said. 'The main reason for opening the first orphan house was to show God's power at work. We thought that if people saw all the needs of the orphans being supplied without any appeals for money they would have to give serious thought to God's power and his goodness.'

Fred looked concerned. 'You mean that you didn't open the homes for the sake of the orphans, but just to show people what God could do?'

Müller shook his head and smiled kindly at the boy. 'No Fred,' he assured him, 'it wasn't like that at all. God laid it on our hearts to help you and those like you. He gave us hearts of love for you and he moved the hearts of thousands of people to provide for you. In doing that he has shown his power and his compassion in the most wonderful ways, not just here but overseas too.'

Relief spread over Fred's face as he rolled over on to his back and basked in the afternoon sun.

'Would you like to hear how The Scripture Knowledge Institution's other aims worked out?' Müller asked the boys.

'Yes please, sir,' Walter spoke for them all.

'Well, we did open day schools as well as a school in which to train our own teachers. And the money we've been given has helped distribute Scriptures throughout the world, to places you've never even heard of in your geography lessons. The Institution supports schools and orphanages in a number of different countries. Mrs Müller and I have visited some of them on our travels. And we've also been able to meet up with many of the missionaries who have been helped by receiving funds from us.'

'Everyone must love you,' said Fred.

Müller laughed aloud. 'My dear boy,' he said, 'there are people who don't like me one little bit!'

Fred horrified at the thought asked 'But why?'

'I'll give you just one example,' the old man said. Because we provide a home at Ashley Down for our boys until they are fourteen or fifteen and for our girls until they are a bit older, some factory owners think that we're cheating them of cheap labour. You see, if they could get you to work in the factories when you are twelve they would have to pay you less. But we don't allow that. So I'm afraid that factory owners in this part of the country don't think as highly of me as you do, dear boys.'

'You're looking very thoughtful, Walter,' Müller said.

The boy looked up. 'Sir,' he said, 'has God always provided enough money?'

'Only two years in more than sixty have the expenses been greater than the income,' the old man explained. 'The first time that happened money came in right at the beginning of the following year. And the second time we were able to borrow from the bank for a very short time on the basis of an extra piece of land we owned.'

'Did that make you doubt God?' asked Fred.

George smiled gently at the boy. 'No, dear boy,' he answered. 'But when money doesn't come in we have to ask why. For example, just last year, 1892, less money came in than before. We prayed about it and it seemed the right time to close some of our day schools at home and to reduce funding going overseas, although the schools there continue and we send money when we can. Situations change, you see, and God provides for the needs of today not for the needs as they were yesterday or twenty years ago.'

Enjoying having Müller as a captive audience, Walter continued with his questions.

'Sir,' he asked, 'will you build more orphan homes here at Ashley Down?'

'Are you a mind reader, my boy?' laughed the old man. 'I can only answer that question because of a decision taken just the other day. We've decided not to do any further building here and that ten-acre plot of land over there will be sold as it is no longer needed. In fact,' he added, 'I was going to take a walk over to it when I was waylaid by five inquisitive young gentlemen about half-an-hour ago.'

Müller rose to his feet. 'And if these five young gentleman would like to join me on my walk they would be most welcome.'

Miss Fletcher looked up just as they set off. 'All boys together,' she said, 'despite the age gap!'

♦ ♦ ♦

On January 13th, 1894, Susannah Müller died. In his sadness, George wrote in his journal, 'My loneliness after sixty-two years and five months of a happy married life (the total of both his marriages) has been and is great; but I continually praise God for what he gave me, for what he has left me for a long time, and for what he has now taken, for it is all good for me. By constantly admiring the Lord's kindness to me in this thing, and that he has now entirely freed my beloved departed one from all bodily and spiritual infirmities, and made me unspeakably happy in his presence; he overpowers my loneliness, and is doing more than merely supporting me.'

♦ ♦ ♦

'I didn't think we'd see much of Mr Müller after his wife's death,' Miss Archer said to her old friend in the summer of 1895.

Old Miss Fletcher laughed. 'You underestimate him. Trust him to give up his home and come to live at Ashley Down! He works as much as ever.'

'And I heard that's he's writing the Annual Report this year again. And I heard something else too.'

Miss Fletcher waited to hear what it was.

'There's going to be a presentation to him at Bethesda Chapel on his ninetieth birthday.' Miss Archer told her. 'What a day that will be!'

'The children have all sorts of plans to celebrate it. They've been making presents and cards, writing letters and drawing pictures. There's no end of the ways they are finding to mark his birthday. But he can't have many more birthdays,' she said sadly. 'How we'll miss him when he goes.'

♦ ♦ ♦

But George Müller lived to be ninety-one and ninety two as well. His ninety-second birthday was in the year in which Queen Victoria celebrated her Diamond Jubilee. The Mayor of Bristol gave a gift of £50 to Ashley Down from the city's Jubilee Fund to mark the occasion.

'How should this money be spent?' James Wright asked.

Müller's eyes brightened up. 'I think we should give the children a treat they will long remember.'

James laughed. 'How typical! And what were you thinking of?'

The old man clasped his hands together and thought for a minute or two. 'Let's take them to Clifton Zoo.'

The others in the room expressed their agreement.

'What fun they would have,' George went on. 'They would see all the animals ... and that would be educational too,' he commented to the teachers present, 'the big cats and the seals and zebras. They'll love the zebras!'

Miss Fletcher winked at her friend and Miss Archer had trouble not laughing.

'And we can have tea there and as many treats as they could want. Do you agree?'

They must have done as the outing to the zoo went ahead.

♦ ♦ ♦

On Wednesday 9th March, 1898, Müller went to bed as usual. When he wakened in the morning he ate the biscuit and drank the glass of milk that had been left at his bedside the night before. Some time between then and 7am, when he was found dead on the floor beside his bed, George met Jesus face to face. The man who had prayed for his every need, met the Son of Man who had prayed for him.

The city of Bristol mourned the passing of its most famous citizen. The children of Ashley Down mourned the only father many of them had ever known.

George Müller's orphans were among those who lined the streets for his funeral. Many fine words were said about him that day, both by politicians and preachers. But the last words in the story of his life should come from an orphan in a letter to James Wright.

'I was so grieved to hear of the death of our dear and honoured father and benefactor. We, the orphans, especially those at present in the Homes, will feel that there is a blank and void that can never be refilled in exactly the same way as dear Mr Müller filled it. We, perhaps, will never know what we have been saved from, or all that has been done for us in the past, present or future, through his life; but God knows, and he who watches over and tenderly cares for the little soulless birds will surely reward the love and care shown to the orphan children so untiringly for so many years.'

Jesus said,
'Let the little children come to me,
and do not hinder them, for the
kingdom of heaven belongs to
such as these.'
Matthew 19:14

Thinking Further Topics

Has reading this book started you thinking? Are you wondering about what you should do with your money? Are you wondering perhaps what Jesus thinks about certain things or perhaps you want to find out about giving your life to Jesus. The following pages will help you think more about lots of issues raised in this book.

Following that there is a prayer diary for you to use. This will help you pray about the issues that are raised in this book as well as helping you focus on God.

Chapter 1
Apprentice thief

By the time George was ten years old he was an accomplished thief and liar. But was he a sinner? If a child does something wrong is he naughty or is he a sinner? Is there a point in the process of growing up when we change from being naughty to being sinners? What is a sinner anyway?

Romans 3:10-12   Among the people we know there are some we think of as good, and others we would say are bad. Are only the 'bad' people sinners?

Genesis 3: 1-15   What gives us the sinful nature that makes us want to sin? What a difficult question! But think of it like this: we inherit our natures from our parents. Our 'first parents' were Adam and Eve. Their natures were affected by the Fall (that's what Genesis 3 is all about). Our inheritance from Adam and Eve is the sinful nature that makes it natural for us to sin.

Does that mean that, because we are sinners by nature, we're not really responsible for what we do? What does Romans 6:23 tell us that sin earns? Do we get wages for what we are by nature or for what we do ourselves? Or is it that we get wages for what we do with what we are? As everyone is born a sinner, and we all go on to commit sin, the first half of that verse could give us cause for despair. But what hope does the second half hold out?

What about punishment, is it an end in itself or a means to an end? At what age should punishment begin to be used, and how should it be administered? And how should Christian parents cope with biblical teaching on punishment (Proverbs 13:24) in a society that sees any form of physical punishment as barbaric and even criminal?

Chapter 2
From bad to worse

When we open a box of chocolates we think we'll eat only one or two. But, having had our favourite ones, we want to try the others. Before long there are hardly any chocolates left. We've even eaten the coffee creams we don't really like! Chocoholics would tell us that chocolates are addictive. Is sin addictive too? Does a little lead to a lot? Is there a progression: try once and find it's not too bad, try again and find we enjoy it, try again because we enjoy it, then find ourselves unable to give it up because it has become part of us? And where do we go from there? Is it to experiment with something else, something a little more exciting and a bit more daring? Do we ever allow ourselves to get out of our depth, and then feel awful when we realise just what we've done?

And how do we feel about people we see doing wrong things? Do our consciences become so accustomed to our own sinfulness that we begin to excuse others theirs? And, if we dabble in something we know is wrong, do we make friends with others who do the same? We make judgments about other people by the company they keep. Are we aware that others do the same with us?

Proverbs 2:12-15   These verses are about delighting in doing wrong. It uses interesting words. It talks about leaving 'straight paths' and walking in 'dark ways'. What are the areas in which we have left the straight way? The opposite of straight is crooked. Is there any crookedness in the way we live?   How can we identify the 'dark ways' in our lives?
Romans 1:32 Does this tell us anything about ourselves and about the relationships our sin leads us into. Do we need to live like that?

Chapter 3
New beginnings

What impressed George about Herr Wagner's meeting was that Herr Kayser knelt to pray. He had never seen such humility.

Psalm 10:3-6   Our sinfulness should make us feel ashamed. But does it? Do we feel bad when we know we've done wrong? Or do we only feel ashamed when we've been found out? According to these verses, what characterises the sinner?

1 John 1:8-9   Do we always mean it when we say 'sorry' or is it sometimes just a word, a way out of a sticky situation? Does saying 'sorry' dent our pride at all? What state of mind and heart do we have to be in to say 'sorry' to God? Jesus told a story to illustrate how we should approach God. See Luke 18:9-14.

1 Corinthians 5:11   When George was converted he distanced himself from his former lifestyle. This verse gives some very practical advice on the subject. What could this involve in our day to day lives? Think of it in relation to the people we associate with,

the places we go to, the programmes we listen to and watch, the books and magazines we read and the films we attend.

Isn't this terribly negative? Can we put it to good effect, by positively cultivating friendships we know are good, and by choosing hobbies and entertainments that are wholesome? Philippians 4:8-9 has something to say to us. Does that seem dull, depressing and 'old'? That's not what it sounds like in verse 4!

Chapter 4
No pay, please

Do we ever feel bogged down in decisions? Christians long to please God, but how do we know what he wants us to do? Older Christians go to the Bible for guidance, but does an ancient book like that say anything relevant to the kind of decisions we've got to make? George Müller found that it did.

2 Corinthians 6:14 God's Word doesn't tell a boy whether he should date that lovely girl with sparkling eyes and a laugh that makes him want to laugh along with her. And it doesn't tell a girl if she should go out with that warm, sensitive and sporty boy. But does this verse give the ground rules?

Exodus 20:12 and Ephesians 6:1-4 Parents! Are they annoying, not understanding what it's like to be a teenager? Were things very different for them when they were young, so different that they really don't know what life is all about for teenagers today? So what? Even if they are annoying (Or are they really trying their hardest and finding us hard going too?) does God lay down the basis for child/parent relationships?

Philippians 4:19 George and Mary Müller trusted God to supply all their needs, and he did. But were they special? Is God interested in our needs? Does he always keep his promises?

The Müllers didn't accept a salary, instead they prayed for their needs to be met, and they were. Is that how we are all meant to live? Should Christians never accept pay? What does Luke 10:7 say? Could it be that God, by leading the Müllers to rely on him for their simple everyday household needs, was preparing them to rely on him totally for the vast amount of money that would be needed for the orphan work, money he could never have earned?

Chapter 5
Bristol's street children

What motivates us to do good? Does a love of Africans in general make us put money in a street collection for famine victims in Somalia or the Sudan, or is it the picture of a starving child that moves us? Do we respond more generously to an appeal for the victims of an earthquake, or to one for the preservation of an ancient building? Is there something in human need that makes us do what we can to meet it? What is it? Find out what moved Jesus to help people. See Matthew 20:34, Mark 8:2 and Luke 7:11-17. Ephesians 5:1-2 gives us a general principle to follow. Galatians 6:10 spells it out in greater detail.

It is often out of the tragedy of human need that great humanitarian work is done. This was true of the abolition of slavery, the ending of the practice of putting little boys up chimneys to clean them and of employing children to work in mills and mines. And it was by the tragedy of the cholera epidemic in Bristol that Müller's heart was moved to open a home for those orphaned by the disease. Is there anything we could do, in a regular and systematic way, to meet a need in our own area, school or society?

Today there are charities for every imaginable cause - and some unimaginable ones too! How do we decide which causes are worth supporting? And how do we go about supporting them? Some charities, for example Tear Fund, have created special opportunities for young people to become involved. Is this something that could be fitted in around schoolwork?

Are there ways in which young people can begin to make a big impact? What about writing to Members of Parliament about issues of concern, eg young homeless people, or the country's overseas aid budget? Letters ARE read and taken note of.

Chapter 6
Pennies from heaven

When we were little, we asked our dads and mums for everything we needed, from a goodnight kiss to a bicycle. And, from all that we asked them for, they gave us what they thought was best for us. This was not always what we had asked for.

Ephesians 4:4-6 tells us something of the Christian's relationship with God. He is our Lord, our God and our Father. We accept that he is Lord and God, that is why we worship him. But what about God as Father? Do we relate to him in that dependent way? Do we take our needs to him - the little niggly ones as well as the earth-shattering ones - knowing that he will hear them and answer them by giving us what is best for us, and for those for whom we pray?

Luke 11:5-13   Here Jesus has some words of encouragement for us.   But what is he encouraging us to do?

1 Peter 5:7   Someone described this verse as prayer in practice.   What could he have meant?

Philippians 4:4-7 Is prayer always about asking for things? Paul tells us in verse 7 of something that comes as a result of prayer. What is it and what does it do?

Matthew 6:9-13 Jesus taught his friends how to pray. Try to work out the structure of that prayer. What's it made up of? Identify the praise, the appeal for God to work in the world, the expression of our needs and desire that they be met (is it needs or wants?), the recognition of what we are in God's eyes and the need to sort out our relationships with others, and the prayer that we might be kept from wrong. Is that the pattern we use in our prayers, or do we bring God a shopping list of wants?

Chapter 7
Ashley Down

Do we believe that God is interested in each one of us? If he is, is he interested enough to be involved in individual lives, or is he just a benevolent force in the world? If we don't think God determines our lives, what does? Is it chance, fate or the stars?

Jeremiah 29:11 What does this verse say about God's involvement? Would we rather be in the hands of a loving and caring God or at the mercy of chance, fate or the horoscope in the latest magazine?

Do we ever feel that life is out of control, that the world around us is spinning so fast that we're only just hanging on in there. Writing out Jeremiah 29:11 and pinning it up where we can see it might be just what we need to remind us that God has plans for us, and that his plans are for our good.

Müller had a letter from a neighbour in Wilson Street pointing out that the noise the children made did nothing for his peace and quiet. George took that as showing him God had a plan that involved moving from Wilson

Street. What came out of that? It could be said that, in the plan of God, the letter was the seed from which Ashley Down grew.

Ephesians 3:20-21   Does this verse really describe God, or has Paul gone over the top? Ashley Down must have seemed like a dream. That splendid building, in its beautiful surroundings, became home to many hundreds of needy children. They were well fed, decently clothed and cared for until they could provide for themselves. For poor children orphaned by cholera, that must have been immeasurably more than they could have asked for or imagined.

Chapter 8
No boxes big enough

Are there prayers we have prayed for so long that we're beginning to wonder if they will ever be answered? Have we prayed for the conversion of someone we love, perhaps a parent, brother, sister or friend, over and over and over again, yet they are still not in the least interested in the gospel? Is it worth going on praying?

Luke 18:1-8 Do we choose the timing for the answer to our prayers, or does God? Can we rush him or slow him down? Would we really want to anyway? After all, God's got the whole world in his hands and it hasn't hurtled off into outer space yet!

Have we prayed with all our hearts for something, and it seems God didn't hear? Perhaps we prayed for healing, and the person for whom we prayed died. Maybe we prayed for exam success, and were disappointed when the results came out. While the Bible assures us that God hears and answers our prayers, it seems that he answers in three different ways. Have you prayed, and found God's answer to be 'yes'? On other occasions has God answered 'no'? Perhaps you've also experienced his 'not yet'.

Psalm 115:1 OK, we've prayed for something, God has answered and that thing has happened. Is it, 'Well done me! God did what I told him. Am I not a good pray-er?' What does Psalm 115 say about that?

Matthew 5:16 Do we like being liked? What does it feel like to be admired, looked up to? Does that make us hold our heads up and walk tall? But is that what Christian service is all about? If anyone could have basked in man's praise, Müller was the man. But did he? And if not, why not?

Chapter 9
Home-goings

Are we ever too young to serve God? Has the lady who is crippled with arthritis, or the man who has suffered a stroke, been invalided out of his service?

2 Kings 5:2-3 Are we too young to serve God? Read the whole chapter to find out the result of what one girl did.

Think of Mary Müller. Did her illness or increasing weakness prevent her being useful to God? During all the years Müller was in Bristol, his wife, Mary, and their friend Henry Craik, worked with him as a team. What comforted him when they died?

John 14:3 and 1 Thessalonians 4:13-18 have something to say about what happens to believers after death. But does believing that someone we loved and who has died is now in heaven, mean that we shouldn't feel sad about his passing?

John 11:1-44 describes the events surrounding the death of one of Jesus' friends. Read verse 35 to find out how Jesus felt. Even though he's now in heaven, Jesus remembers that day and that feeling. When we are bereft, Jesus remembers and he understands.

Being a Christian makes a difference when people are alive, but it also make a huge difference when they die. How do you feel when a believer dies? Does the fact that person has gone to heaven comfort you in your sadness? Is it different when a nonbeliever dies, and you don't have that assurance? Think how difficult it can be for a minister taking a nonbeliever's funeral service. Although God can work in the last few minutes of a person's life (Luke 23:39-43) a minister can't hold out false hope to those who mourn. The best he can do is tell them that Jesus offers them a way to eternal life.

Chapter 10
Wedding Bells

How many marriages do you know that have failed? Why did they fail? There might have been unfaithfulness, or perhaps people let their marriage dry up and they became bored with each other. Drink or violence may have been contributory factors too. Should we expect the divorce rate to continue rising? Is marriage breakdown normal and inevitable? How would we react if a friend who became engaged confided in us that she found comfort in the fact that if the marriage didn't work out divorce was an option? Each year we are reminded that a dog is for life not just for Christmas. Is the marriage of a husband and wife seen to be less lasting than the relationship of a dog with its owner?

Genesis 2:22-25 and Mark 10:7-9 What do these verses tell us about the origins of marriage? Who established the first marriage as the pattern for family life? Was it Adam and Eve or was it God?

Ephesians 5:21-33 On what relationship is marriage modelled? What does the Bible say here about love, submission and respect?

And what is submission anyway?

Matthew 5:31-32   Divorce is now so common that we accept it without thinking. But what does Jesus teach about the grounds for divorce?

Death breaks the marriage tie, leaving the surviving partner free to marry again. George Müller and James Wright both married for a second time after the deaths of their first wives. And both their second marriages were happy and used in God's service. What does this tell us about love and marriage? Is it only for the young and beautiful?!

Chapter 11
200,000 miles
in seventeen years!

How do we feel when we have to pass on a job to someone else, a job that we've enjoyed and had satisfaction in doing? Do we watch the other person critically, looking for mistakes? Do we feel resentful when they change our way of doing things? Or do we accept that the time has come for us to move on to something else, and leave that job to whoever has taken it over, giving any help and advice we're asked for?

2 Samuel 7. King David had a great desire to build a magnificent temple for the Lord. He thought about it and dreamed about it. It seemed to him to be the pinnacle of his achievements.

But what did God say to David through Nathan, the prophet? See 2 Samuel 7:12-13. Imagine how David might have felt then read his response (2 Samuel 7:27-29).

And what a job King Solomon, David's son, made of the temple! 1 Kings 7:13 - 8:21

describe the building work. But David was not forgotten. Read 1 Kings 8:24, part of Solomon's prayer at the dedication of the temple.

George Müller, when he was an old man, travelled 200,000 miles in God's service. How do we feel about old people? Should they realise the inevitable: that they've done their thing, made their contribution to society, and now is the time for them to go out to grass? Is there retirement from Christian service? Or do older Christians collect their pensions and go on serving God?

Joel 2:28. What does this verse have to say about the young and the old? On whom is God's Spirit poured out? Does God entrust young and old with exactly the same experiences of himself? And does he pension old people off, leaving only the young to serve him on earth?

Chapter 12

Face to face with Jesus

If we were given an entire new wardrobe of clothes and asked to dispose of our old ones, what would we do? Would the best old ones go to our friends, the next best ones to the charity shop, and the oldest ones to a group collecting clothes for Eastern Europe? Should people who are in real need be expected to make do with not only what is second hand, but what is also second rate?

Visitors to Ashley Down often commented on how well groomed and tidily dressed the orphans were. Because they'd had a bad start, people expected them to wear poverty like a badge all of their days. Was that how Müller felt? Or was his aim to give them the very best, spiritually, physically and emotionally? What were his guidelines for doing that? See Proverbs 22:6, Ephesians 6:4, James 1:27 and James 2:14-17.

George's life was one of preparation. God took him as a teenager, well on the way to a criminal life, and changed him. Year by year he became more like his Lord until, when he died, he met Jesus face to face and was changed into the image of his Saviour. Are we Christians? Has God changed us, and is he making us more like Jesus day by day? George was a very old man when he died, but not everyone is. Are we ready to meet our Creator? If we died now, would we go to heaven?

John 14:1-4, Philippians 3:20-21, 1 Thessalonians 4:13-18 hold some precious promises to those whose faith and trust is in Jesus.

John 3:16-18 is a word of hope and challenge and promise to those who are not yet Christians.

My Prayer Diary

The Bible says, 'Devote yourselves to prayer, being watchful and thankful. And pray for us, too' Colossians 4:2-3.

In this section here write down the names of those people you want to pray for every day. They may be your family and your special friends.

My Family and Friends.

Write down the names of your minister or church leader and those people who help in church life like Sunday School teachers, Youth workers etc.

Write down names of people who especially need your prayers. They may be missionaries, or people doing other difficult jobs. They could be people who are old or ill or who are feeling lonely. Write down a person for every day of the week and pray for them every week on this day.

Sunday

Monday

Tuesday

Wednesday

Thursday

Friday

Saturday

After having read this book let's pray to God about some of the things we have learnt and about specific issues that have arisen in the book.

Pray for those people who make the laws and decisions that affect you and your country.

Government

Let's thank God for the laws and decisions made in Government. Thank him for those leaders and members of parliament who try to help children and protect them. We should pray that more people in parliament will stand up for children's issues. Let's pray that laws will go through to protect children who are living in poverty or in difficult family situations.

Children's Societies

We should thank God for organisations like Save The Children, NSPCC, Dr. Barnardos and other organisations who support disadvantaged children throughout the world. Pray that people will continue to support these worthwhile causes. Thank God too for his own special love for children and for you.

Pray for your country and the other countries and tribal communities that make up your world

Your Country

Thank God that we live in a country that, by and large, takes care of children and protects them. Thank God for all the blessings you have had as a child. Thank God for schools and education. Thank him also for the special provision made for children in hospitals and other places.

Pray for children in our country that do not have the care and protection they need. Pray for those who have lost their parents or who live in poverty with very little help or support from adults. Pray for members of the social services and police who try to help children who are living in bad homes or whose parents are too poor or sick to look after them properly.

Remember to pray for other countries where it is very hard to live and survive as a child. Pray for the third world where many children die from poverty and disease. Pray that Christians will be able to gain access to these countries to share the good news of Jesus Christ. Let's pray that these countries will learn to respect children and young people and that poverty and hardship will soon be tackled in a meaningful way.

Pray specifically. Be informed about your world and nation.

Specific Issues

If you read a newspaper or watch the news remember to pray about specific problems you hear or read about.

Pray about refugee children.
Ask God to protect those children who are trying to escape from countries that are at war. Pray that they will be welcomed to new homes and protected. Let's pray that the adults who are in charge of so many countries will try and learn to live in peace so that the children of their countries can grow up in a safe and secure environment.

Pray about families
So many families suffer from divorce or separation. God wants families to stay together and hates to see the pain and sorrow that sin causes to family life. Pray for friends who may be going through a difficult time after a divorce. Ask God to comfort them. Pray that families who are going through difficult times will realise that God is always there for them and ask God for help.

Christian Church

Pray for the Christian Church. Pray that Christians will read God's word. We should ask God to remind Christians that they have to become just like little children before they can truly say that they are following God. 'Unless you change and become like little children, you will never enter the kingdom of heaven.'

Pray that people in churches will be welcoming to children and that children won't feel left out or ignored. Ask God to help children understand what people talk about in church. Thank him too that the good news of Jesus Christ is so simple anyone can understand it and believe in Jesus.

When you pray it is good to remember to do four things: **Adoration** - this means tell God how much you love him and how special he is. **Confession** - tell God about the things you have done wrong and how sorry you are. **Thanksgiving** - give thanks to God for all the good things he has given you. **Supplication** - this word means to ask. Ask God for the things you need. You can ask him for other things too because he is always willing to give good things to us. Most importantly ask him to forgive you for the wrong things you have done. Ask him to come into your life and be in charge.

The first letters of these four words spells out Acts. So whenever you pray remember this word Acts and you should remember the four things you should do.

TRAIL BLAZERS

A Voice In The Dark
Richard Wurmbrand

by Catherine Mackenzie

'Where am I? What are you doing? Where are you taking me?' Richard's voice cracked under the strain. His heart was pounding so hard he could hardly breathe. Gasping for air he realized - this was the nightmare! Thoughts came so quickly he could hardly make sense of anything.

'I must keep control,' he said out loud. An evil chuckle broke out from beside him. 'You are no longer in control. We are your worst nightmare!'...

When Richard Wurmbrand is arrested, imprisoned and tortured, he finds himself in utter darkness. Yet the people who put him there discover that their prisoner has a light which can still be seen in the dark - the love of God. This incredible story of one man's faith, despite horrific persecution, is unforgettable and will be an inspiration to all who read it.

ISBN 1-85792-298-0

The Watch-maker's Daughter
Corrie Ten Boom

by Jean Watson

If you like stories of adventure, courage and faith - then here's one you won't forget. Corrie loved to help others, especially handicapped children. But her happy lifestyle in Holland is shattered when she is sent to a Nazi concentration camp. She suffered hardship and punishment but experienced God's love and help in unbearable situations.

Her amazing story has been told worldwide and has inspired many people. Discover about one of the most outstanding Christian women of the 20th century.

ISBN 1-85792-116-X

The Storyteller - C.S. Lewis

by Derick Bingham

C.S.Lewis loved to write stories even as a small child. He grew up to face grief when his mother died, fear when he fought in the First World War and finally love when he realised that God was a God of love and that his son Jesus Christ was the answer to his heartache.

C.S.Lewis brought this newly-discovered joy and wonder into his writings and became known world-wide for his amazing Narnia stories.

Read all about this fascinating man. Find out why his friends called him Jack and not his real name. Find out what C.S.Lewis was really like and discover how one of the greatest writers and academics of the twentieth century turned from atheism to God.

"A good introduction to my stepfather C.S. Lewis"

Douglas Gresham

ISBN 1-85792-423-1

An Adventure Begins
Hudson Taylor

by Catherine Mackenzie

Hudson Taylor is well-known today as one of the first missionaries to go to China but he wasn't always a missionary. How did he become one then? What was his life like before China? In this book you will meet the Hudson Taylor who lived in Yorkshire as a young boy, fell desperately in love with his sister's music teacher and who struggled to gain independence as a teenager. You will also travel with Hudson to the Far East as he obeys God's call to preach the gospel to the Chinese people.

Witness the excitement as he and his sister visit London for the first time, sympathise with the heartache as Hudson leaves his family behind to go to China and experience the frustration as his sisters wait for his letters home.

Do you want to know more? Then read this book and let the adventure begin.

ISBN 1-85792-423-1

From Wales to Westminster
Martyn Lloyd-Jones

by his grandson
Christopher Catherwood

'Fire! Fire!' - A woman shouted frantically. However, as the villagers desperately organised fire fighting equipment the Lloyd-Jones family slept. They were blissfully ignorant that their family home and livelihood was just about to go up in smoke. Martyn, aged ten, was snug in his bed, but his life was in danger.

What happened to Martyn? Who rescued him? How did the fire affect him and his family? And why is somebody writing a book about Martyn in the first place? In this book Christopher Catherwood, Martyn's grandson, tells you about the amazing life of his grandfather, Dr. Martyn Lloyd-Jones. Find out about the young boy who trained to be a doctor at just sixteen years old. Meet the young man who was destined to become the Queen's surgeon and find out why he gave it all up to work for God. Read about Martyn Lloyd-Jones. He was enthusiastic and on fire for God. You will be, too, by the end of this book!

ISBN 1-85792-349-9

Look out for future titles
in the series:

Isobel Kuhn

Look out for our

New Fiction Titles

Twice Freed
Patricia St. John

Onesimus is a slave in Philemon's household. All he has ever wanted is to live his life in freedom. He wants nothing to do with Jesus Christ or, the man, Paul, who preaches about him.

Onesimus plans to make his escape one day. He gets his chance in the middle of an earthquake. After he manages to steal some money from his master Onesimus sets off for a life of freedom. Along the way he meets friends and enemies and fights for his life as a gladiator in the Roman arena. Will Onesimus escape? Will he one day find his way back to Eireene the beautiful young merchant's daughter? Find out what happens and if Onesimus realises the meaning of true freedom!

ISBN: 185792-489-4

Look out for our

New Fiction Titles

Something to Shout About
Sheila Jacobs.

Jane is back in her old home town of Gipley but things are not the same as they were, in more ways than one. Heather's mum has got a slimy new boyfriend, Heron introduces everybody to her very good-looking brother, Woody, and it seems as though Heather's church is now going to get closed down. Woody persuades Jane and Heather to spear head a 'Save our Church' campaign. Soon the girls are up to their necks in banners, slogans and campaign strategies. However nobody has thought to ask God what he thinks of the whole situation. Eventually Jane learns a valuable lesson about prayer and seeking God's will in every situation.

ISBN: 1-85792-488-6

CHRISTIAN FOCUS

Good books with the real message of hope!

Christian Focus Publications publishes biblically-accurate books for adults and children.

If you are looking for quality Bible teaching for children then we have a wide and excellent range of Bible story books - from board books to teenage fiction, we have it covered.

You can also try our new Bible teaching Syllabus for 3-9 year olds and teaching materials for pre-school children.

These children's books are bright, fun and full of biblical truth, an ideal way to help children discover Jesus Christ for themselves. Our aim is to help children find out about God and get them enthusiastic about reading the Bible, now and later in their lives.

Find us at our web page:
www.christianfocus.com